The Charisma
Effect

Prentice Hall LIFE

If life is what you make it, then making it better starts here.

What we learn today can change our lives tomorrow. It can change our goals or change our minds; open up new opportunities or simply inspire us to make a difference. That's why we have created a new breed of books that do more to help you make more of *your* life.

Whether you want more confidence or less stress, a new skill or a different perspective, we've designed *Prentice Hall Life* books to help you to make a change for the better. Together with our authors we share a commitment to bring you the brightest ideas and best ways to manage your life, work and wealth.

In these pages we hope you'll find the ideas you need for the life *you* want. Go on, help yourself.

It's what you make it

* * *

The Charisma Effect

How to make a powerful and lasting impression

Andrew Leigh

PEARSON

Prentice Hall

LIFE

Harlow, England • London • New York • Boston • San Francisco • Toronto
Sydney • Tokyo • Singapore • Hong Kong • Seoul • Taipei • New Delhi
Cape Town • Madrid • Mexico City • Amsterdam • Munich • Paris • Milan

PEARSON EDUCATION LIMITED

Edinburgh Gate
Harlow CM20 2JE
Tel: +44 (0)1279 623623
Fax: +44 (0)1279 431059
Website: www.pearsoned.co.uk

First published in Great Britain in 2008

ISBN: 978-0-273-71721-8

British Library Cataloguing-in-Publication Data
A catalogue record for this book is available from the British Library.

Library of Congress Cataloging-in-Publication Data
Leigh, Andrew.
  The charisma effect : how to make a powerful and lasting impression / Andrew Leigh.
    p. cm.
  Includes bibliographical references and index.
  ISBN-13: 978-0-273-71721-8 (alk. paper)
  1. Self-presentation. 2. Self-perception. 3. Interpersonal relations. I. Title.
  BF697.5.S44L45 2008
  158.2--dc22

                          2008012184

10 9 8 7 6 5 4 3
12 11 10 09 08

Typeset in 10/14 Plantin by 30
Printed and bound in Great Britain by Henry Ling Limited, at the Dorset Press,
Dorchester, DT1 1HD

The publisher's policy is to use paper manufactured from sustainable forests.

Contents

About the author

Andrew Leigh is a founding director of Maynard Leigh Associates, the development and consultancy service whose mission is to unlock people's potential.

For some years he was a business feature writer on *The Observer* and later worked for many years as an Assistant Director in the public sector. Author of more than a dozen books on management, leadership and presentation, he is a Fellow of the Chartered Institute of Personnel and Development.

Acknowledgements

The Charisma Effect reflects contributions from various people who have kindly read drafts, commented or assisted in some way. In particular, I am grateful to:

- Henry Stewart of Happy Ltd who helped set the whole idea in motion;
- the following from Maynard Leigh Associates: my fellow Director Michael Maynard, for his usual full and thoughtful observations; Bridget Brice, Director of the Personal Impact Course; Adrian Jones, Ann Walsh, Barbara Thorn, Bill Britten, Caroline Kennedy, Deena Gornick, John Spencer, Josie Maskell, Rosanna Mason, Steve Bolton and Siobhan Stamp;
- and from outside Maynard Leigh: Roger Taylor of T-Mobile, Ian Cutler of Skandia, Susan Coulson of Barclaycard, Simon Adams and Aiden Leigh.

Thanks also to Darion and Aiden Leigh for their technical help with the charisma-effect.com website.

Samantha Jackson of Pearson Education nursed this book from inception to its final publication and was always a support throughout.

Finally, I offer special thanks to Gillian Leigh who, despite her busy schedule, went far beyond the call of duty by providing many insightful improvements and suggestions.

The Charisma Effect is dedicated to Gilly.

Publisher's acknowledgements

We are grateful to the following for permission to reproduce copyright material:

Unnumbered figure on page 17 © Maynard Leigh Associates 2007, reprinted with permission; Unnumbered table on page 176 Copyright © 2005 Mitch Ditkoff, Dave Pollard, Tim Moore and Carolyn Allen, reprinted with permission; Box entitled 'Hot words of influence' on page 197 adapted with permission from Shelle Rose Charvet (1997) *Words That Change Minds: Mastering the Language of Influence*, 2nd edition, Kendall/ Hunt Publishing. www.WordsThatChangeMinds.com.

In some instances we have been unable to trace the owners of copyright material and we would appreciate any information that would enable us to do so.

Introduction: unravelling charisma

'The minute you walked in the joint, I could see you were a man of distinction. A real big spender.' This lyric, famously belted out by diva Shirley Bassey, is a musical reminder that people judge us in an eye blink. It stems directly from charisma, or lack of it.

The purest form of charisma occurs with larger-than-life characters like Ghandi, ex-president Bill Clinton, Nelson Mandela, Madonna, Oprah Winfrey, Mohammed Ali, Churchill, Mother Teresa and Archbishop Desmond Tutu.

Nor can we entirely ignore the negative version. Hitler, Stalin, Idi Amin, Mao and Mugabe all mobilized it with lethal results. Charisma and 'good' do not always coincide.

> charisma and 'good' do not always coincide

We are so used to the word charisma that we seldom spend any time thinking about why most of us view it in the way we do. Not understanding our charisma DNA or our unconscious perception of it can limit our potential to use it positively.

The conventional view of charisma assumes only a few, exceptional people possess it. It seems to imply mysterious, almost magical, properties and that you are either born with it or not. However, as we shall see, it is not entirely innate and relies on creating a relationship between you and others.

Possessing strong charisma often brings to mind a historical figure, a celebrity, a powerful leader or a creature of fame. It is never entirely clear which is cause and which effect.

In many ways, it feels comfortable to view charisma as beyond reach, safely reserved for those exceptional human beings we are destined to admire, envy or perhaps fear. Yet does their super charisma mean that the rest of us cannot have a significant and memorable impact on people we encounter. Certainly not.

This convenient notion that charisma is beyond reach allows us to exclude ourselves from any serious attempt at owning up to our potential to make a powerful and lasting impact. That we might truly be powerful, able to significantly influence or affect others can seem impossible, terrifying or both.

Another aspect dominating how we view charisma is that it usually involves large numbers of people. Celebrity entertainers, great religious and spiritual leaders, high-profile politicians, military geniuses are all examples of exceptional charisma that affected large swathes of humanity.

Yet for all their extraordinary impact, supreme exponents of charisma remain human beings. While impressive and even puzzling, their effects are not magical, supernatural or even unobtainable. To some degree, each of us can produce a diluted version, called the Charisma Effect.

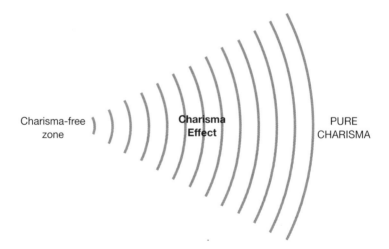

This effect is entirely learnable. It is about tapping into your natural ability to make a powerful impression, even if this currently lies dormant or under-exploited. Your personal impact *is* your Charisma Effect, and the two terms are used interchangeably throughout this book.

In claiming you can improve your impact I am not entirely alone. Others also report success at developing this capability, though they may put a slightly different emphasis on how to do it. For example, one interpretation argues it happens through using energy and becoming fully present. These are certainly important ingredients, but it is rather more involved than that, and certainly takes time to develop.

On and off stage

When the curtain rises for a stage play we instantly begin making judgements about the various characters, trying to make sense of what is happening. Real life is less simple, there is no rising curtain. Instead, we can find ourselves performing without always knowing when we are on, or off, stage.

Famously, Marilyn Monroe was out shopping with a friend who was amazed that no one seemed to recognize the star. Monroe explained it was because at that moment she was off stage, and to demonstrate, 'switched on' her star quality. Within minutes, she was mobbed by people asking for her autograph.

Apply for a job and you may believe you are off stage because the interview has not yet begun. Yet the curtain goes up even before you press on the buzzer or walk through the door, and it is up when you talk to the receptionist, as you sit waiting, when you shake hands or perhaps while you sit reading before the interview starts.

Chairman of UK's Royal Mail, Alan Leighton, recalls an experiment in one company where he traced the progress of about

50 people over a 10-year period. At a relatively young age they had progressed from junior positions to just below board level. 'The nearest thing we found to a common denominator was the first impression of the senior manager in the room when they recruited them – the gut feel. And that became part of the criteria that we recruited on – the first impression.'

Similarly, when working in an office where everyone, including you, seems quietly absorbed, you may imagine no one is taking much notice, and you are off stage. In practice, without them fully realizing it, people are aware of you and your behaviour. Whether you like it or not, you are on stage.

> whether you like it or not, you are on stage

So, your impact on other people matters. What they think about you can make a big difference to your life, affecting your relationships, whether at work or at home, at a local committee meeting, at a parent–teacher session, making a complaint to a shop and so on.

Your impact is your personal currency, almost entirely dependent on how effective you become at mastering the Charisma Effect.

Most people want to convey a favourable first impression that others will enjoy and remember. Even more, most of us would be delighted to communicate with confidence and leave a good lasting impression. Well it is entirely possible.

You can choose to develop how you come across and do it naturally, without seeming false or appearing to be manipulative. I am going to share with you some of the methods from our work teaching and coaching people to achieve these results. Quite simply, we are going to start exploring your unique Charisma Effect.

This effect is the secret of being a success with other people, gaining their agreement, confidence, commitment or admiration. Those exhibiting it strongly tend to be congenial and comfortable when interacting with others. They also possess the ability to influence: we talk of them as having charm, and the magnetism to connect, physically, emotionally, intellectually and perhaps even spiritually.

The Charisma Effect...

... is the ability to use all aspects of yourself to achieve a strong, memorable impact on other people, influencing them emotionally, physically and intellectually, including their thoughts, attitudes and behaviour.

In the more traditional sense, pure charisma is usually defined as being an unusual ability to influence people and arouse devotion.

Throughout this book I will introduce you to the ingredients that help create your Charisma Effect, not the extreme version of pure charisma. Of course, not everyone will agree with these ingredients since even today this remains an under-researched area. I can only say that many people have found these helpful from our Personal Impact workshops and in the one-to-one sessions we have run for many years for many major corporations.

Traditionally, people expect their political leaders and heads of large companies to be larger-than-life characters. At one annual company meeting, attended by the up-and-coming Stuart Rose, who went on to run Marks & Spencer, an investor brutally asked the chairman: 'Why aren't you charismatic like Stuart Rose?'

Recent studies reveal a significant difference between possessing and using pure charisma to bedazzle and seduce people, and simply using the less demanding Charisma Effect to get results. As one of the most respected researchers in this field explains, 'Less charismatic leaders often produce better long-term results than their more charismatic counterparts'.[1] Collins' seminal study of successful leaders found surprisingly that great corporate leaders

[1] Collins, J. (2001) *Good to Great*, Random House.

are 'self-effacing, quiet, reserved, even shy – a paradoxical blend of personal humility and professional will. They are more like Lincoln and Socrates than Patton or Caesar.'

'You don't necessarily have to be charismatic,' confirmed the late Dame Anita Roddick, founder of The Body Shop, 'you just have to believe in what you are doing so strongly that it becomes a reality.' Putting this slightly differently, in the crude showbiz sense, the extreme version of pure charisma can be a liability, which is why the focus here is on the more achievable Charisma Effect.

While you may be happy to improve your Charisma Effect, some of those around you might prefer you to stay the same. It is a bit like losing weight: while it may be entirely beneficial, others might actually prefer you plump and comfortable. So when it comes to actually changing, be prepared to meet resistance, if not in yourself then possibly from others.

The early part of this book explores your aims and their impact on how you come across to people and the impression you make. The second part shows how, through natural behaviours, you can really be yourself while affecting how people experience you. The third part dissects the difficult area of chemistry, through the relationships you create with other people.

The final part brings it all together to show how you can use chosen parts of the approach to modify and enhance your Charisma Effect to create a powerful and lasting impression.

Whenever you have an impact on another human being, you will be using your own version of the Charisma Effect. It is working for you each time you succeed in influencing a group, a team, a boss, a colleague or anyone you encounter. This book aims to help you develop this natural ability further. Throughout it you will find a series of practical work outs that will help hone your self-awareness and give you practice in various aspects of using the Charisma Effect.

this book aims to help you develop this natural ability further

You may decide to read the book from start to finish and that is fine. Equally you may prefer to home in on an area that you already know you need to develop. Apart from a readiness to experiment with new ways of behaving what matters most is your willingness to accept that you can indeed develop your Charisma Effect with some of the various forms of help available.

The people factor

Even the most fanatical hermit, devoted techie, fixated computer geek, besotted specialist or focused manager must, to some extent, deal with other human beings. Interactions between us and other people generally form a normal part of daily life, whether in meetings, seeing the boss in the corridor, talking to a client, having a job interview, making a phone call or being in a team. And what all those people think of us matters, because their opinions and reactions affect how they respond to us and what we want.

Come across well to other people and they will tend to listen to you, notice what you say, seek your views, respond to your requests and so on. When achieving a strong impact you are not merely present, you convey a positive presence. The process involves these three key elements:

Because sometimes one element influences the other and vice versa, the interactions can become complicated. For example, you may visit your neighbour with a certain intention, only to alter it in response to the reaction you encounter. Or, when you propose an idea to your family that provokes a big reaction, this may make you modify your original idea in some way.

In virtually any interpersonal situation where you want to create a powerful and lasting impression, the A-B-C approach provides a series of easy to recall landmarks. The combination of these three elements will ultimately determine the strength of your Charisma Effect and we sum up the whole process visually like this:

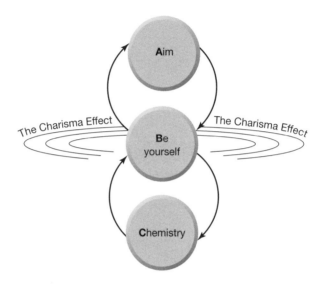

Think of the Charisma Effect as being like ripples in a pond. Some will be extremely strong, pushing far outwards, while others have more modest localized effects.

The ripples from our Charisma Effect lead people we encounter to make judgements about us. Often these occur so rapidly that is it surprising that countless popular magazines bombard us with advice on such basics as appearance, style and what colours to wear? Yet they deal with only the more obvious aspects of the Charisma Effect in action; there are also less obvious ones which we will be exploring together.

When was the last time you were at your best and made a strong impression? Try completing the impact work out overleaf and see whether this reveals anything interesting about your current impact on others.

Impact work out

1 Briefly describe a time when you felt you made a really good impression on someone or a group of people

2 Where did this occur?

3 List some of the reasons it went so well (e.g. smiled a lot; rehearsed; remembered everyone's name).

4 How did you feel at the time (e.g. confident, relaxed, curious, ready, determined)?

Looking at what you have written, what does this reveal about your personal impact?

If you have trouble identifying when you made a really good impression think about a time when you got a job, had a romance, met people on holiday, completed a project and so on. Perhaps you can also recall a time when you felt:

● 'They didn't really listen to me.'
● 'I couldn't get my point of view across strongly enough.'
● 'I didn't feel confident in that situation.'
● 'They never really saw the real me.'
● 'We just weren't on the same wavelength.'
● 'I don't do small talk.'

- 'I feel uneasy talking to senior/older/important people.'
- 'I really wish I'd made a stronger impression.'

It can be frustrating to watch others make an impact, communicate their ideas or convey their opinions or needs with apparent ease. Yet there is nothing secret about achieving a Charisma Effect. It only seems that way because many people simply do not realize that there are methods and principles which can be learned and applied.

Unfortunately, those who do possess a strong Charisma Effect often seem the least able to explain how they do it. To them it may come naturally, so they cannot readily offer help to ordinary mortals wanting to develop their own version. So, together we are going on a journey, exploring the A-B-C of the Charisma Effect, and how you can make a positive impact in a wide range of mainly informal or small group situations, such as one-to-one meetings, work discussions, conversations with people you encounter, group or team sessions, phone conversations and so on.

> unfortunately, those who do possess a strong Charisma Effect often seem the least able to explain how they do it

For most of us informal situations will be more familiar than, say, a stand-up presentation or delivering a conference speech. While only a select few mount a speaker's platform, we all regularly engage in informal communications that challenge us to make the right kind of impact.

Rigid rules on how to make a positive impact seldom really work. Consider the less than sharp appearance of Microsoft's Bill Gates, the studied casualness of Richard Branson, the cheeky chappie style of London mayor Ken Livingston. You would hardly say they conform to so-called rules of good grooming. Yet they have an undeniably strong Charisma Effect.

Being you is enough

You are a one-off, a unique personality. If you attempt to act like Madonna, pretend to be Mandela or even copy your own boss to make an impact, you will probably crash and burn. This is why the A-B-C approach has a major focus on being yourself. You can simply adapt it to meet your particular needs in various situations.

Research suggests charisma is half innate and half learned. Certainly, we have used many of the ideas in this book during our long-running Personal Impact workshops and our evidence suggests virtually everyone can unlock their potential to access their natural Charisma Effect. Companies such as Aviva, Bertelsmann, SES Astra, Bank of Ireland, BMW, Fidelity, DHL, Electronic Arts and Ernst & Young, have all used these workshops at some time.

You can deliberately choose to develop your Charisma Effect and the main requirement is deceptively simple—it is your willingness to:

● experiment.

Experimenting does not mean you will become an entirely different person or alter your basic personality. You will still be you, though you may feel a new sense of confidence after trying new ways of behaving.

Developing your Charisma Effect is about your willingness to experiment with new ideas, to explore new behaviours, to find ways to raise your self-awareness about the impact you actually make. Jacqueline Gold, persuasive head of the Anne Summers chain of shops sums it up succinctly: 'Challenge yourself and great things will happen.'

It can be tempting to assume you will only start applying some of the ideas and suggestions in this book once you have read it. That is rather like one of our participants on our Personal Impact workshop who was asked some weeks afterwards how it was going and who replied: 'Well, fine, but I haven't had a chance to use it yet.'

To develop your Charisma Effect you need to keep working at it, to find daily ways to practise and experiment. You can do it wherever you have contact with other people, on the phone, in a shop, with friends at a restaurant, travelling, in meetings, around the drinks machine, anywhere. Once you get the hang of making an impact you will find countless opportunities to put it to work. To test your readiness to experiment, see the mirror work out below. If you are travelling and reading this on a train or a plane, I suggest you put the book away until you can complete the work out in privacy!

 ## The mirror work out

You will need:

- a watch with a second hand or digital counter
- a largish mirror you can physically hold in front of you
- a quiet place in which to be without distraction for a while.

Here is what to do next.

1 For five whole minutes, examine yourself in the mirror! No cheating, just keep looking and looking and looking. What do you see?

2 While looking, keep your mind alert. What do you see beyond your familiar features? What do you see in those staring eyes? What is your expression? What sort of character does this person you are looking at seem to have?

3 What would someone else particularly notice about this individual?

Did you manage to do the mirror work out for five whole minutes or did you give up sooner? If you abandoned it prematurely, why did it seem so long or difficult? If you did give up early, take a break now and perhaps try again – for the full five minutes. This time be particularly aware of your own reactions during the activity.

If you succeeded for the full five minutes what did you see? You, of course, but what else? Who was this person looking out at you? What did you notice about this person? What stood out? Was this a happy or a sad person?

Incidentally, you can watch the mirror work out amusingly brought to life with its self-awareness-raising potential in the 2005 film *Angel-A* by Jean-Luc Besson.

Why do it?

Why do this apparently narcissistic work out? After all, you probably look at yourself in the mirror every day; maybe even spend quite a bit of time making yourself appear groomed or more attractive. The mirror work out is about getting to know yourself even better, raising your self-awareness, increasing your ability to 'see' and interpret signs and information.

So what kind of person stared out from the mirror? Was it a serious person, a person who constantly smiles or frowns, a person who looks happy, sad, angry or worried? What can you tell about this person just by looking at them?

 Charisma Effect work out

You probably have your own ideas about what contributes to a person coming across strongly or not.

1 Choose someone who impresses you with an ability to create the Charisma Effect; that is, to achieve a noticeable, strong personal impact. Choose someone you know, rather than some distant celebrity figure such as TV personality, sportsperson or movie star.

2 List all the things about them that you feel produces their Charisma Effect.

Name of person: ....

What is it about them contributes to their Charisma Effect? Why do they seem to make a positive and lasting impression?

For example, they are direct, challenging, charming, etc. Be as specific as you can.

- ....
- ....
- ....
- ....
- ....
- ....

3 How many of the attributes about this person concern their actual behaviour and how many can be explained by intangibles such as personal chemistry?

A

Aim
You are meeting for a reason.
Be clear what your aim is –
what do you want to achieve?

B

Be yourself
Take your whole self with you
to the encounter. Remember
your sense of quality.

C

Chemistry
Listen, respond and seek partnership.
You will be more likely to achieve
your aim if the chemistry is right.

ABC of the Charisma Effect

'It is never too late to be what you might have been.'

George Eliot, writer

Part 1

Aim

Discover and clarify your real purpose

This first part of our A-B-C approach to developing your Charisma Effect explores ways to strengthen your self-awareness, shows what it means to be a chooser rather than a victim, offers reality checks on your personal impact and suggests ways to sharpen up your Charisma Effect aim.

Chapter 1

Aim

Strengthening your Charisma Effect starts with raising your level of self-awareness – that is knowing:

- who you are and what you stand for
- the effect you have on others
- the effect others have on you
- what is happening around you.

Raising self-awareness may sound daunting but the mirror work out (see page xx) was a start in that direction, making you more alert as to who you are and what others see in you.

You are being self-aware when you:

- can look at yourself coolly and objectively, and can probe and analyse the whole person, warts and all
- accept other people's evaluation of you without becoming defensive or fearing a threat to the core of your being.

Developing your self-awareness, particularly what you are trying to achieve with your Charisma Effect, plays a large part in creating a positive personal impact on others, which is why it is so is important.

For example, with a high level of self-awareness you will know what you want to say or indeed that you have nothing to say. You also

you will know what you want to say or indeed that you have nothing to say

become comfortable asking for feedback on your performance and can handle negative criticism. You will tend to receive such information as comment on what you do, rather than who you are.

Character work out

Inside each of us we have various characters that we allow to surface in different situations. How aware are you of these? You might have inside you, for example, a gambler, a bully, an action hero, a joker, a tease, a thinker, an organizer, a charmer …

1   Who are some of your own inner characters?

2   When do these characters tend to surface – is there a trigger for their appearance?

3   What happens when they do surface, how do you tend to behave?

4   How do you think they affect your impact and how you come across to others?

Raising your self-awareness affects your impact on others because you start playing to your strengths, minimizing any weaknesses. You see how your behaviour affects others and realize how they respond. Most of all it means being able to speak openly and accurately about your emotions.

There are plenty more ways of raising your-self awareness as shown throughout this book.

Which one are you?

If setting out to raise your self-awareness still makes you feel positively uncomfortable it could be that you have a tendency to be one these:

- poor me
- blamer
- observer.

All three are essentially victims, things happen to them and they are constantly on the receiving end of events, rather than making choices and being proactive.

The poor me victim

This victim type tends to be deep into self-pity, saying things like:

- 'I don't have a strong personality.'
- 'If only I was prettier/better looking/taller/shorter/cleverer.'
- 'I've never had a strong speaking voice.'
- 'I may be the manager, but nobody listens to what I say.'
- 'I'm not good at talking to others.'
- 'I can't handle small talk.'
- 'It takes a long time for people to get to know me.'
- 'Why don't people see I'm a nice person?'

- 'I'm no good in groups or teams.'
- 'People don't like me.'

Poor me victims seldom say outright they cannot improve their Charisma Effect or strengthen personal impact. Instead, when offered the chance to do so they seldom follow it up.

For example, they are reluctant or even refuse to hear critical feedback, listening only to unstinting praise. The poor me victim finds challenging personal feedback unsettling, grossly unfair or both. They also have a habit of interpreting comments or remarks by others in the worst, rather than the best, possible light.

The blamer victim

Blamers always manage to find something or someone to criticize for their weak Charisma Effect. They say things like:

- 'Nobody considers my opinion.'
- 'My company doesn't appreciate me.'
- 'The loudest people get heard.'
- 'I never got on with my parents/brothers/sisters.'
- 'The school I went to was terrible.'
- 'Nobody ever showed me how.'
- 'There's never enough time to get myself across properly.'
- 'It's because of my accent.'
- 'I just don't have enough seniority.'

When it comes to boosting their Charisma Effect, blamers usually fail to see new possibilities or new ways of changing how they come across.

Warning signs that your Charisma Effect needs attention

- 'I don't feel people really listen to me in meetings.'
- 'I get offered jobs or projects below my level of ability and training.'
- 'I hate, fear or feel uncomfortable about giving a presentation or a talk.'
- 'I feel uncomfortable looking people straight in the eye when I talk to them.'
- 'People often ask me to repeat what I have said.'
- 'People fidget, interrupt or look away when I speak.'
- 'I have trouble getting my ideas accepted.'
- 'In informal situations requiring small talk, I feel tongue-tied and awkward.'
- 'People often tell me I've picked the wrong time or place to raise a certain subject.'
- 'Whenever people offer me advice or suggestions, they usually say "yes but...."'
- 'I often feel on the defensive with people.'
- 'I find it hard to get others to co-operate with me.'
- 'I don't really care about having a high profile, it's substance that counts.'
- 'I have trouble remembering people's names, even after I've just been introduced.'
- 'I'm not a joiner, I'd rather be alone.'
- 'In meetings I like to sit where I won't be much noticed.'
- 'When I enter a room I tend to hesitate, walk slowly and keep my head down.'
- 'My facial expressions do not usually match my feelings.'
- 'I feel I have impact but it is not always the one I want.'
- 'I find it hard to make decisions, I have lots of self-doubt.'

If one or more of these apply to you, read on!

The observer victim

The observer is the final type of Charisma Effect victim. When it suits us, we all occasionally play this role. For example, we are being an observer when we remain determined to stay above the fray, refusing to lower our guard, never removing the mask.

Staying objective and unemotional may make perfect sense yet observers become victims through the unusual frequency and intensity of their standing back. They say things like:

- 'I'll keep my head down.'
- 'I'll stay cool and see how things work out.'
- 'Let others make all the noise.'
- 'I'll save my breath.'
- 'Watch and wait is my motto.'
- 'I like sitting on the fence.'

Dedicated observers seldom make the first move, often using silence as a weapon. Deliberately or without realizing it, they leave a communication black hole, into which they expect others to fall. They also respond defensively to any communication initiative directed at them, making it hard for the rest of us to know what they think or to build a relationship with them.

Really shy people can feel comfortable being observers even though they realize it minimizes their Charisma Effect. When invited into a conversation, for example, they prefer to hang back and let others do the hard work.

> they leave a communication black hole, into which they expect others to fall

Many people in business, while not particularly shy, play the observer because they mistakenly think this will give them power and avoid any personal risks. So, for example, they sit in meetings in a defensive posture, perhaps with arms folded and defy everyone else to make them say something. They assume they are showing gravitas by staying silent and aloof.

Being an observer can be useful but not if you turn it into a near permanent way of being. That way you become a negative force, excluding yourself from influence and hence becoming a victim.

Do you have any observer tendencies? If so, you will probably be hard to read as a person. Others may struggle to discover what you think about something or even whether you have an opinion at all. Perhaps without realizing it, you relish the mystery created by playing observer and enjoy the power of being a human riddle.

 Victim work out

At your next meeting, at work or elsewhere, do the following.

1 Take a special interest in watching and listening to what individuals say and do.

2 Can you spot any signs of them playing poor me, blamer or observer?

3 What did they say or do to reveal they were in victim mode?

4 How did others react to these individuals? What did the victims do and how did they look?

5 What feelings does this victim behaviour arouse in you – for example did you feel sorry for the person, annoyed, angry or frustrated?

From victim to chooser

It is not much fun being a victim and it does terrible things to your Charisma Effect. If you think you have any of these victim tendencies it is time to start moving from being a victim to a chooser.

We can all be victims occasionally and the source of our victimhood may lie far in our past – in family, school or other experiences that have left us feeling in some way inadequate, unwanted or unheard. Naturally you do not simply give yourself a good shake and instantly eliminate such feelings. Deep-rooted causes and their consequential victim behaviour may sometimes make it difficult to change. Yet there is always a first step, which in this case means starting to act like a chooser, someone who looks for and seizes opportunities to explore your Charisma Effect in action.

> welcome tough feedback and deliberately use it to start doing things differently next time

For example, if you do not make the kind of impact you want, instead of simply blaming others or feeling hurt decide that this time you will welcome tough feedback and deliberately use it to start doing things differently next time.

A more active form of chooser seeks opportunities for testing out their charisma effect, for example, grabbing the chance to give a presentation, even though the very thought of it may be repugnant. Or rather than as usual plunging in with opinions, instead wait to be asked for suggestions or ideas. Yet another way of becoming a chooser is to create entirely new situations where you can put your Charisma Effect to work, perhaps by devising a new project or piece of work where you can shine and raise your profile, or making yourself known to others in a new situation without waiting to be introduced and so on.

You can find out more about the victim and chooser models at www.charisma-effect.com. Look under the 'Resources' menu item.

First impressions

In our daily lives, many of us choose to don a mask, not allowing others to see the real person underneath. Sometimes it is a victim mask, but it may also take the form of an unreal persona that allows us to face a difficult world. For example, someone who insists 'everything is under control' when it manifestly is not is wearing a mask. So too are those people who when asked 'How are you?' blandly reply 'Just fine' when the reverse is obviously the case.

The mask conceals what we feel behind it, hiding our fear of what people might actually see, such as our sense of inadequacy or our uncertain communication aim. On this journey of enhancing your Charisma Effect you will need to explore what your particular mask looks like and what lies behind it. Try the behind the mask work out.

 Behind the mask work out

1   Consider how you would *like* to be seen by others.

2   In the left-hand column below write five to eight descriptions, for example, happy, tough, punctual, thorough, dedicated, funny, honest, organized, clever, thoughtful, cheeky, bubbly. Give careful thought to the ones you choose.

3   Next consider how you *fear* you come across to others. For example, might they see you as ruthless, ambitious, funny, careless, rude, clumsy, late, immature?

4   Review the two lists together. What do they reveal about your likes and fears? How accurate do you think they are? Which attribute is the one you would most want to be linked with? And which is the one you would least want? Are there any surprises?

How I'd like to be seen   How I fear I'm seen

....

....

....

....

....

....

....

5   How accurate do you think the two lists you made really are?

Because they experience you in real life, other people can provide you with an important reality check. For example, you may feel you come across as quiet and thoughtful, while those who meet you might describe you as aloof. Or you may believe you are funny and superficial, while those who meet you have a different perception.

To obtain more reliable data on how you come across to others consider using the fast reality check out or the personal impact profile described overleaf. These both require you to actually approach people to find out how they experience you. This may feel horribly embarrassing but you do not need to ask people you distrust or those you personally dislike. Instead choose people from your inner circle before tackling anyone outside it. Remember, there is nothing shameful about wanting to strengthen how you come across to people.

> remember, there is nothing shameful about wanting to strengthen how you come across to people

After you receive back the completed questionnaires, add up the values shown by the ticks in each row and produce a single total. The maximum score possible is 70 (7 $\times$ 10).

Divide your score by 70 and multiply by 100 to reach your personal impact (PI) index. For example:

- your score is 45
- the maximum possible is 70
- your PI index = 45/70 $\times$ 100 = 64%.

Scores over 75% suggest you have a good personal impact and should probably concentrate on building on your particular strengths further. Scores under 75% suggest you would benefit from working on selected areas of both strengths and weakness.

Now review the answers to the two open-ended questions posed at the end of the check out. Can you identify any patterns or common themes in the various answers?

Fast reality checkout

I am exploring the personal impact I make on people – that is, how I come across to you. Please be as frank as possible, scoring me on a 10-point scale by ticking one box for each attribute.

| | Low | | | | | | | | | High |
---	1	2	3	4	5	6	7	8	9	10
FLUENCY – speaks fluently and well										
CONFIDENCE – willing to accept alternative views, open to challenges, not defensive, able to be spontaneous										
PRESENCE – intensely alert to the present situation, shows gravitas, maintains good eye contact, demonstrates stature and substance										
AUTHENTICITY – true to oneself, not putting on a front, reliable and dependable										
COURAGE – willing to be different, to challenge and question, to think outside the box, to take risks										
PASSION – shares personal values, is energized, openly committed, enthusiastic, engages other people										
DEMEANOUR – physical bearing, well turned out, always looks stylish and distinctive										

What do you think works well about how I come across to you?

....

....

What do you think works less well about how I come across to you?
(Be honest, I won't get upset – promise!)

....

....

There is no single best way to achieve a strong Charisma Effect, for example, always smiling, having a noble bearing, maintaining eye contact or talking eloquently. Instead, it emerges from blending a unique mixture of behaviours or traits that are like colours on an artist's palette.

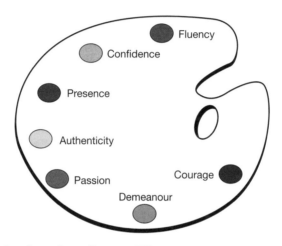

The artist's pallete of your Charisma Effect

When people encounter you face to face, what do they most experience? What behaviours or 'colours' of your Charisma Effect seem to work best for you, and in what combination and situation? Which of these would you use most and which the least:

● fluency

● confidence

● presence

● authenticity

● courage

● passion

● demeanour (well turned out, stylish and distinctive).

Your personal impact profile

For a more in-depth way of assessing your personal impact consider using a more thorough online system, which allows you to collect more detailed, anonymous information from colleagues, and compare this with your perceptions about yourself.

For example, using the Maynard Leigh online system produces a personal impact index score out of a maximum possible of 100. While most people never achieve this ultimate result, we normally expect someone with a good Charisma Effect to score at least 70–75%. A sample profile for Frank Sinatra is shown below.

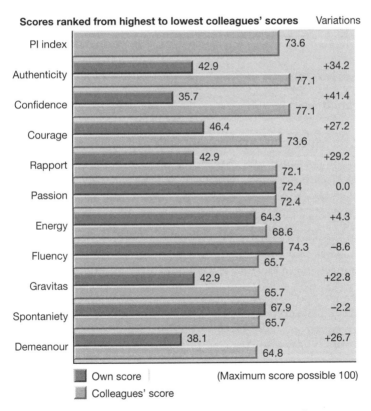

Scores ranked from highest to lowest colleagues' scores · Variations

		Variations
PI index	73.6	
Authenticity	42.9 / 77.1	+34.2
Confidence	35.7 / 77.1	+41.4
Courage	46.4 / 73.6	+27.2
Rapport	42.9 / 72.1	+29.2
Passion	72.4 / 72.4	0.0
Energy	64.3 / 68.6	+4.3
Fluency	74.3 / 65.7	–8.6
Gravitas	42.9 / 65.7	+22.8
Spontaniety	67.9 / 65.7	–2.2
Demeanour	38.1 / 64.8	+26.7

■ Own score · (Maximum score possible 100)
□ Colleagues' score

The big picture: profile chart for Frank Sinatra (not the singer!)

Source: © Maynard Leigh Associates 2007, reprinted with permission.

If you would like to try this more challenging profile free, there is more information at the end of the book.

If you do not have a wonderful Charisma Effect profile there is no sense in punishing yourself, few others have one either. It is merely a device for answering important questions such as:

- How do others see me?
- Is my perception of how I come across aligned with how others experience me?
- What should my Charisma Effect aim be? What do I most need to communicate?
- What are my Charisma Effect strengths and what are my development needs?

Sharpening up your aim

Dylan Moran, the youngest person to win the UK Perrier Comedy Award in 1996 and who appeared in various films, including *Run Fat Boy Run*, wants to make you laugh. His 2006 zig-zag tour of Britain, New York and Milan was described by *The Times* as a 'master class of comic charisma'. Comedians like Dylan with a big personal impact know exactly the effect they want to achieve. Making their audience laugh is their prime concern; it is where all their energy, creativity and attention is focused. For example, they may spend quite a lot of time assessing the different audiences they have to encounter so they can tailor their act accordingly.

> every communication situation you encounter involves an aim and an audience

Like Dylan, whether at work or outside it, every communication situation you encounter involves an aim and an audience. People with a strong Charisma Effect usually evolve their own preference for which matters most – deciding the aim or defining the audience. Naturally both matter but the exact order may not be critical. Since we are using the A-B-C approach to personal impact we start with **aim**.

Think of just about anyone with a really strong Charisma Effect and it is usually obvious that, like Dylan Moran, they have made up their minds as to what impact they want to have. With politicians it is all about selling their vision or offering alternative ways of spending our taxes. With certain media people their aim is merely to entertain and be provocative. With company managers the aim may be to motivate, raise awareness or trigger action.

Clarity first and last

If you have only vaguely defined communication aims this may partly explain why you do not always achieve the effect you deserve. For example, being unclear about exactly what you want from a one-to-one meeting with your boss can send mixed messages and cause confusion. Likewise if you stand up at a presentation without knowing what result you want to achieve then it is likely your impact will be seriously diluted.

Try treating the whole aim issue like telling an adventure story.

● Aim: what does the hero want to achieve?

● Obstacles: what might stop the hero achieving the aim?

● Solutions: how does the hero overcome these obstacles?

Aim ⟶ **Obstacles** ⟶ **Solutions**

Sales people know this sequence well as they work towards discovering customer objections and coming up with ways to overcome them. Good presenters follow this sequence as they work to clarify what they want to say and how to break through audience inertia or resistance.

People with a strong Charisma Effect become skilled at choosing their communication aim, even if they do not always put it that way. Consciously or otherwise they set specific goals and imagine how others will react to them. They select the messages and behaviours they believe will make them personally effective.

the more explicit your headline the easier it will be to deal with obstacles and solutions

An essential part of every aim is the basic requirement to build some kind of relationship with those affected. This is the difficult area of personal chemistry, with which we deal later.

Choose a headline

Adopting a single headline to describe your communication aim can further sharpen up your intention. In one succinct sentence describe what you want to happen at the end of an encounter. For example, your basic aim might be to:

- persuade people they can trust me
- get them to give me my money back
- win commitment to some specific action
- gain approval for my ideas
- make two new contacts
- inspire people with my enthusiasm
- get them to listen to me with respect
- raise my personal profile.

Each of these states a definite result in a single sentence. For example, my single headline aim in writing this book is:

To show you it's perfectly possible to develop your Charisma Effect.

The more explicit your headline the easier it will be to deal with obstacles and solutions. Focusing on the precise result you want from any encounter makes you clarify your aim. For example, the end outcome for a forthcoming meeting might be:

- a warm smile and handshake at the door
- a commitment to start the project next Tuesday
- new volunteers come forward
- agreement to meet again next month.

Notice the results are specific, not generalities. This prevents you from thinking of the Charisma Effect as something done *to* people, rather than achieving a desired result.

Try the clarifying purpose work out shown below. Obviously, you would not complete this analysis for every single communication situation you face, but when you really want to unleash your Charisma Effect this kind of thinking can make it easier to achieve.

Clarifying purpose work out

1   Complete the empty table below as follows.

● Write down a specific situation at work where you want to have a greater impact. It could be in a team meeting, talking with your boss, meeting a client, on the phone etc.

● What is the specific result you want to achieve? Try to see it from the other person's point of view – what's in it for them?

● Describe what a 'win' would look like, sound like and feel like?

Complete the table in as much detail as you can.

Situation for making an impact	What specific result do I want?	What would a 'win' look, sound and feel like?
Example: Our regular team meeting.	*Example:* For people to listen to my ideas and take them seriously.	*Example:* When I suggest something in our team meetings the other members actually discuss it and I feel treated with respect.
Now add your version here.		

2   How clear is your intent? Could it be still clearer?

In selecting your communication aim try using the CAN DO criteria. For example, does your headline communication aim meet these five simple criteria:

- **C**lear: Short enough to write as a simple headline.
- **A**chievable: One you feel is attainable.
- **N**eeded: Something you really want to achieve.
- **D**ivisible: Can be broken into smaller aims if necessary.
- **O**utcome: Explains what success would look, sound and feel like.

Use the CAN DO criteria whenever you have a really important personal impact aim to achieve.

Smaller, secondary aims can directly or indirectly steer your behaviour and therefore your eventual impact. For example, suppose you have to enter a room filled with people standing around already chatting. Your overall headline aim might be:

> I want to make at least five new business contacts.

While this is a perfectly sensible and specific aim, you must still face that daunting room of people chatting, oblivious to your presence. If you are also someone who is nervous or shy you may find it more manageable, for example, to use these secondary aims:

> *Enter*: walk in as if this is my party and these are my guests. *Smile*: go up to five individuals or groups and introduce myself. *Ask*: 'Are you having a good/useful time?' *Invite*: my party guests to tell me about themselves and their business. *Collect*: ask five people to exchange business cards with me.

The secondary aims can be particularly helpful when planning a talk, a stand up presentation, sales pitch or other more formal encounters.

Secondary aim work out

1   Choose a personal impact aim you feel is important to achieve.

2   Write it down as a single headline sentence.

3   Review whether it meets the CAN DO criteria of Clear, Achievable, Needed, Divisible into secondary aims, with definite Outcomes. If not redefine it.

4   List some additional secondary performance aims – make sure each aim has a clear result that you can assess afterwards.

Obstacles

Most aims will probably encounter some kind of obstacle along the way. For example, you may wish to impress your boss with the idea of a new project yet your boss is not someone easily impressed. Or you may want to get your whole team to take some action, but the members tend not to listen well to new ideas.

You cannot deal with all the possible obstacles that might stop you achieving your aim, as that would probably stop you doing anything at all. Instead, identify the three or four main ones that could really get in the way. As in the previous work out, it may be helpful to describe what a win–win situation would look, sound or feel like, for both you and those on the receiving end of your communication. What obstacles might stop this happening?

Solutions

How would you know your solution has worked and your obstacle has been overcome? For example, will people stand up and applaud, will people start taking your ideas seriously, what signs will appear to show that communication obstacles have been dealt with successfully?

if you are finding it hard to produce solutions this should prompt you to further refine your aim

If you are finding it hard to produce solutions this should prompt you to further refine your aim. For example, rather than try to surprise your not easily impressed boss with the idea of a new project, you may decide your aim will become: 'To excite her with the possibilities of personal advancement if she takes on this project.' Or, with your family who tend to all talk at once, rather than propose some desirable action, your first aim might be: 'To make everyone realize there is a problem that needs tackling.'

Keep it simple

Try reducing your desired aim to a single verb that describes the effect you want to achieve, for example:

> My aim is to: inform, amuse, alert, discover, motivate, shock, enrol, encourage, warn, sell, build, excite.

Our bodies carry our aim, often without any conscious effort on our part. Focusing on your aim can help you have a greater impact naturally. Your aim lets your body speak for you.

Since how you come across happens through your body, not just your words, it is vital that your physical performance matches whatever intention you choose. Saying, 'This is an exciting opportunity for our team, let's fully grasp it', while speaking in a dreary monotone and staring down at the floor will not work. Or, declaring how extremely sorry you are about some serious situation while smiling and looking cheerful would also not be effective.

When your Charisma Effect aim closely matches how you feel inside, it will almost certainly strengthen your impact. As we will see in Chapter 5 being authentic is one of the essential ingredients of a strong Charisma Effect.

Visualizing the aim

Defining your aim is so important that here is yet another powerful way to bring it alive. In this approach, you devise a story of the exact outcome you want, with a beginning, middle and an end, seeing it like a movie running in your head.

Suppose you have been invited by e-mail to join an exciting new project and want to win your manager's agreement. The mental movie of your aim might run something like this:

Beginning

- I smile broadly as I enter the manager's office.
- I sit down in the usual chair.

Middle

- She listens with interest.
- I tell her about the project's benefits to her and the company and she keeps saying 'yes' lots of times.
- When I see her smiling or nodding, I pop the question about a possible start date.
- She readily agrees to a start date.
- I smile my thanks.

End

- I get up to leave still smiling.
- As I reach the door I turn to say goodbye.
- I see her smiling at me.

It does not matter if this an entirely likely scenario – for example, you know in reality your manager hardly ever smiles, let alone listens with interest.

You do not need to be a particularly visual person to create these kinds of mental scenes. You simply daydream! Let your mind gently construct the story in bits and pieces, until something emerges describing what you want to happen.

the more you play with the mental scenario, the more you can adjust it

The more you play with the mental scenario, the more you can adjust it to align with your aim. This constant visualizing of the aim as a movie can help you clarify what you want to achieve and it can directly affect how you behave, your body language and therefore your Charisma Effect. Don't knock the mental movie until you have tried it; it can really work!

Keep running this mental film in your head, imagining the outcome you want. See it in black and white, in colour, as a silent movie, as a fly-on-the-wall documentary. Even 'watch it' just before entering the room to meet your manager.

Multiple aims

So far we have used one main headline aim to analyse in detail, but in real life you may be juggling with several entirely different headlines. For example, you might want to make not only a greater impact on your boss but also raise your profile in your team, build a long-term relationship with a client and gain agreement from a colleague for something. While all these aims can be compatible with each other, they may make it hard to focus your Charisma Effect energies. In trying to achieve them all, you may not make enough impact across all of them. Since multiple headline aims can be distracting, try to prioritize them.

1   List each of your main headlines.

2   Rank each in terms of importance from highest to lowest.

3   Select the highest-ranking aim to achieve first, do the second highest one next and so on.

Personal impact aims	Ranking (1 = highest)
Greater impact with boss	1
Raise profile in the team	2
Build relationship with client	3
Get agreement from colleague for new project	4

'I always wanted to be somebody, but now I realize I should have been more specific.'

Lily Tomalin, actress

Part 2

Be yourself

The seven Charisma Effect behaviours

This next part of our A-B-C approach to developing your Charisma Effect deals with seven essential behaviours:

- fluency
- confidence
- presence
- authenticity
- courage
- passion
- demeanour.

Each of these directly affects how you come across.

This part offers ways to adjust and develop these behaviours, so you become more effective in your interactions and make the impression you want.

Chapter 2

Fluency

I want that glib and oily art', demands Cordelia in Shakespeare's *King Lear* after realizing she is not being persuasive enough. People with a strong Charisma Effect tend to be articulate and whether you call it oily art or the ability to talk well, personal success within, and often outside, many organizations usually demands a certain way with words.

This is not solely about public speaking – though this may be important – being fluent at work is now almost mandatory.

> being fluent at work is now almost mandatory

To enhance your Charisma Effect you may need to develop your facility with words, phrases, ideas, values, issues, feelings and general communication.

While the research is open to challenge, the evidence suggests words alone play a minor role in how we come across to others. Non-verbal aspects can be far more important.

Since communication is a two-way affair, what you transmit also needs to be received by the other person. You will only be fully articulate when those on the receiving end absorb your message.

● If they haven't heard it, you haven't said it.

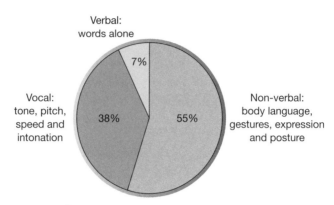

Verbal:
words alone

7%

Vocal:
tone, pitch,
speed and
intonation

38%

55%

Non-verbal:
body language,
gestures, expression
and posture

How we communicate

Being fluent at speaking can certainly improve your Charisma Effect, as the impact of David Cameron's speech at his party conference in 2007 showed. Many people were impressed at his apparent ability to speak for over an hour without a script, hardly glancing at his notes. Yet he did not really need them, because his main focus was on his audience, not the words.

As Shakespeare's Hamlet told his band of actors, 'Suit the action to the word, the word to the action.' Being fluent means matching your words to your action and this we explore more fully in Chapter 5. It also requires you to:

- speak with ease
- explain complicated ideas simply
- communicate convincingly
- bring your message to life
- speak clearly and audibly
- use silence appropriately and powerfully.

Speak with ease

Your use of language instantly tips people off about how educated, competent and effective you are. Numerous studies show a strong link between success and a good vocabulary. Most of us, however, use only a fraction of the vast stock of available words.

> most of us, however, use only a fraction of the vast stock of available words

Having a large vocabulary is fine, so long as you can readily call on it when needed. Merely knowing lots of words, though, is far less important than being able to put together your message so people find it worth listening to in the first place.

You need to be able to speak without repetition or hesitation. For example, how are you with those security blanket 'ums', 'aahs' and 'ers'? If you tend to pepper your speech with these then you need to start practising to eliminate them. The trouble is that we often do not even realize the extent to which we rely on these verbal delaying tactics. This is yet another reason to check out with the people you trust just how reliant you have become on these props.

Shakespeare solved the problem of having a ready supply of words by inventing nearly 2,000 of them. Dylan Thomas and James Joyce did the same when it suited them! A slightly less creative way is to steadily massage your vocabulary.

- First check out your vocabulary to assess how good it is. You can do this at a vocabulary tester such as www.javacamp.org.

- Learn one new word each day and within three months you will acquire and use nearly a hundred new words. You can even receive a new word with its definition and sample sentences daily. Visit http://dictionary.reference.com.

- Linkage: see how words link to others at www.visualthesaurus.com.

- Sentence completion: have fun with word completion and vocabulary tests at www.majortests.com.

- Read: make yourself encounter words you do not already know and find out what they mean by reading well-written books that challenge your vocabulary.

- Take classes: explore subjects like art, music, theatre, literature, languages, philosophy, science and psychology that offer new ways of looking at and expressing ideas.

- Listen: take every opportunity to listen to individuals who express themselves well – avoid relying on politicians, athletes and other celebrities, most of whom parrot trite phrases.

- Conversation: find ways to get involved in thoughtful, mentally challenging conversations.

Explain complicated ideas simply

'Great leaders are almost always great simplifiers, who can cut through argument, debate, and doubt to offer a solution everybody can understand', commented US General Colin Powell. Because the average human attention span lasts just 15 seconds or less, we need to learn to get our messages across quickly. Almost anyone can make a subject complicated, even how to make a good cup of tea – the official UK guidance on this runs to six pages!

> almost anyone can make a subject complicated, even how to make a good cup of tea

People with a strong Charisma Effect realize the importance of reducing complexity and ruthlessly simplifying their message so what they say lands easily. For instance, few people really understand biotechnology but that does not prevent the best scientists such as leading theoretical physicist, futurist and TV presenter Dr Michio Kaku from talking about it so most of us can broadly understand what is involved.

Some of the worse anti-simplicity offenders tend to be highly committed professionals who thrive on, and even reward, obscurity. With this in mind, financial services company ING Direct deliberately recruits non-bankers able to challenge the status quo. It recognizes that familiarity leads to myopia and subject-matter experts who rarely view things the way customers do.

Simplifying complicated ideas means giving jargon its marching orders. While jargon can be a useful shorthand between fellow professionals, it may also reduce personal impact, even amongst knowledgeable colleagues.

● Avoid jargon if you want to simplify.

Another way of simplifying is to explain the 'big idea'. You cut through technical complexity to show what lies behind an issue or problem. The film director Cecil B. De Mille once summed up his proposed blockbuster film of Samson and Delilah for Paramount officials as: 'Boy meets girl – and what a boy, and what a girl!'

For a while, super simplification conquered Hollywood and everyone pitching ideas for a movie was expected to do it in a few words or sentences.

● Girl meets girl and they drive off a cliff.
● Martians conquer the world but die from a virus.
● A sweet little fish loses its parents and finds them again.

Try the simplification work out overleaf.

Simplification work out

Just for fun, and because it will help you practise aiming for the big idea, see
how many of the following films you can explain in one short sentence.

Film	Explanation
The Matrix	
Lord of the Rings (any one film)	
The Godfather	
Pulp Fiction	
Jaws	
The Terminator	
Alien	
Fight Club	
Wuthering Heights	
Pretty Woman	

Alternatively, choose half a dozen films you know well and use them to write
your one-line summary.

Communicate convincingly

When the government's chief scientist sits opposite the UK's prime
minister and says the country needs to expand its use of nuclear
power, he carries more weight as an independent adviser than, say,
the head of British Nuclear Fuels Ltd pushing for exactly the same
thing. However, being convincing only partly relies on your role or
job. Studies of successful leaders in highly profitable companies

confirm that many of them do not have a particularly strong Charisma Effect, yet they still manage to sound convincing.

Apart from clarity of purpose (see Chapter 1) and non-verbal factors (see the chapters on chemistry in Part 3) other factors that play an important part in helping you sound convincing are conviction – the strength or passion behind your communication – and message content.

Conviction

When people share their passion or enthusiasm for something it is catching and helps convince people. Tap into your own conviction by starting with what excites or interests you about your message.

If you are unconvinced by what you want to say, why should others be the opposite? Try breaking your message into smaller parts to see if you can uncover some aspect of it that fully ignites your interest or enthusiasm. For example, suppose you must talk to customers about your company's new product yet you feel unenthusiastic about it. Rather than hoping for the best, find some aspect about this product, no matter how small, that you do see as interesting or convincing and focus on that.

● To convince others, first convince yourself.

Content

Although actual words are a minor part of sounding convincing, the contents of your verbal messages can potentially affect credibility.

● Do you present enough facts to support your case?
● Is what you say logical and easy to follow?
● Is the content sufficiently brief for people to absorb it?

For example, in a job interview, to avoid sounding merely boastful can you support your previous experience with solid evidence? Are there examples, statistics, expert references or even testimonials to support your case? Or when discussing some issue with your boss,

underpin your opinions with facts and tangible evidence

do you always include solid facts to support what you say, rather than mainly relying on assertion? In a team meeting, underpin your opinions with facts and tangible evidence. Beefing up your content in this way may mean more time on preparation than you currently allow, but inadequate preparation tends to be a killer, especially with formal presentations.

Being logical and easy to follow will strengthen your impact on others. Not only are most people's attention spans short, people can usually only remember two or three points made during a verbal interchange. For instance, the actual order in which you present information matters.

● A foundation stone for sounding convincing is to give people the most important information first.

Bring your message to life

Fluent people often enliven their impact using creative phrases. 'We're still dancing', claimed Chuck Prince as head of Citibank when talking about possible board differences. A memorable visual image can be an important part of building one's Charisma Effect.

Claiming that the seemingly impossible is possible – namely a better world – Professor Hans Rosling ends his now famous presentation at the TED conference, seen by over 500,000 people over the Internet, by swallowing a large steel sword.[1]

Metaphors and similes

Metaphor and similes paint memorable pictures in people's minds, describing something as *if* it were something else. They help explain

[1] Visit www.gapminder.org.

conceptual ideas, convey complex notions and provide a shared understanding, allowing us to use verbal shorthand. Example metaphors are:

- 'This family has rock solid values.'
- 'There are a few rotten apples in that team.'
- 'We've got to bust the speed limit on this one.'

You may associate metaphors with poetry, literature and art, yet we all use them, often unconsciously, during daily conversation. Because they are so effective at quickly conveying tangible and conceptual information they are woven into the fabric of our English language. When Chief Executive Lee Iacocca was trying to rescue Chrysler he carefully did not ask the US government for a 'rescue package' but instead talked about a 'safety net' to prevent the company having to fire many people.

Similes use 'as' or 'like' to compare something to something else, for example:

- 'He's as hard as nails.'
- 'She's as tough as old boots.'
- 'Turns up here on Tuesdays like clockwork.'

If you have an idea or a message you want to get across to colleagues, try choosing an object or an action that is completely unrelated. For example, suppose you want to sell your team the idea of a new activity, and also enjoy whitewater rafting – what connections can you make between the two? Making them, however tenuous, may produce some memorable and persuasive phrases.

Speak clearly and audibly

We are so used to hearing our own voice that we tend to pay little attention to how we sound when we speak. This is because we have lots of casual, low-level communication and mainly get by. Our friends seem to understand us easily and accept who we are and how we sound, but to achieve the Charisma Effect requires attention to what we say and how we say it, and that includes:

- diction – whether you pronounce words and sentences clearly or not
- pitch – how high or low your voice goes
- volume – whether or not you can be heard
- tone – what mood your voice conveys, such as friendliness, anger, etc.
- pace – how fast you speak.

Diction

One reason why people do not speak clearly is they are not carefully checking that their message is landing, which is why eye contact can actually help with diction.

> eye contact can actually help with diction

Check if you speak clearly by being brave enough to obtain feedback. One way is to record yourself speaking and listen with a critical ear for whether or not your speech is clear, crisp and easy to follow. Alternatively, during a conversation you might ask if the other person finds you speak clearly. This may be a bit daunting but it will give you the information you need.

You can also try these ideas.

- Watch yourself talking in the mirror—what are your first impressions of your speaking voice?
- Practise enunciating your words. Demosthenes the Greek orator improved his clarity of speech by putting a pebble in his mouth until he could be understood, despite its presence. Rather than risk swallowing a pebble, try placing a pencil horizontally in your mouth to force you to enunciate your words more clearly. (Be careful not to choke on it though!)

● Practise talking more slowly. Giving your words an extra
second or two to leave your mouth can really help with your
personal impact. Pausing also works because it allows your
listener to digest what you have said (see also page 47).

Speaking clearly is so important that, while you can certainly
tackle this on your own, it may also be helpful to spend some time
with a specialist voice coach.

 Voice work out

1 Smile broadly while you read the paragraph below:

   'This team is doing really well, we have surpassed all our targets and are on
   track for a record-breaking month. Well done!'

2 Now read the same paragraph while you frown and tighten your jaw.

3 Note how your facial expression changed the sound of the message

Pitch

People with a weak Charisma Effect are often unaware that they
talk in a monotone. Boring voices occur for several fairly common
reasons: dreary content, over-reliance on a written script and a
voice pitch that sounds wooden – that is, unmusical.

Reading your presentation aloud is a guaranteed way to sound dull
and reduces your voice to a charisma-sapping drone. Even great
actors find it challenging to speak an entire script and make it
sound interesting.

To vary your pitch, make sure you move your body! It works!
Other ways include the following.

● Breathe more deeply, and relax.

● 'Lean' on important words and phrases, putting energy into them.

● Inject more emotion into what you say.

● Emphasize the ends of statements and questions.

Again this is a tricky area of personal development where a qualified voice coach can quickly help you to achieve a more varied and interesting delivery.

Volume

Entrepreneur Karen Darby, a big personality who sold her price comparison website SimplySwitch for £22 million, speaks 'like she is making sure she reaches the cheap seats, even though there are just two of us sitting in the small room', commented the *Guardian* in October 2007. In contrast, Dorothy Parker, the famous US writer and humourist, deliberately spoke so quietly that to catch her words people had to lean towards her. They were rewarded with brilliant satirical wit that generated her particular impact. In choosing to talk so quietly, she knew exactly what she was doing, projecting just enough to hold people's attention.

> talking either too loudly or too quietly can undermine your Charisma Effect

Talking either too loudly or too quietly can undermine your Charisma Effect so it is worth checking out if you currently have the volume control too high or low. Do people often ask you to speak up or repeat yourself? If they do, it probably indicates you have rather a quiet voice, even though it may sound perfectly normal to you.

 Strengthen your voice work out

1 Stand up straight. This enables your lungs to expand to their full capacity and your diaphragm to be unrestricted.

2 Take a deep breath and fill up your lungs.

3 Speak as though the air is coming from your stomach.

4 Speak evenly, not letting all the air go into one phrase and resulting in a wild yell. Having taken a nice deep breath, you will have the benefit of plenty of air to sustain you through an entire steady sentence.

It takes a while to perfect the technique so give yourself plenty of practice.

If you are worried you might suffer from a strident or harsh voice, watch for signs such as people withdrawing from you, even if only slightly, or perhaps wincing as you talk. Alternatively, be brave and ask some trusted colleagues for direct feedback.

 Using loudness work out

1   Speak each of the following sentences softly.

 ● I didn't say that!

 ● Leave me alone.

 ● Give it to me.

 ● Get out of here.

 ● I want it now.

2   Then using the size values of each word in the sentence as a guide, increase volume with word size.

 ● I didn't say that.

 ● Leave me alone.

 ● Give it to me.

 ● Get out of here.

 ● I want it now.

Note how the meaning of what you say changes with the volume.

Tone

Tone conveys whether you are being friendly, angry, cheerful, patient, etc. and can play an important part in establishing your personal impact.

No matter how relaxed he tried to appear, ex UK prime minister John Major's public voice always sounded alien and strangulated. It is hard to appear cheerful, confident or persuasive if your voice says to your listeners, 'Can you hear how tense I am?'

To create a rich, creamy tone involves using your diaphragm, your vocal cords and the amount of sound resonating in your throat, mouth and head. I know it sounds a bit complicated, which is why having training from a voice expert can really help.

For a simple tone work out, try the one shown below. If you feel it does not help, consider looking for some outside support. This might include visiting a qualified voice coach, someone with a professional qualification in this area. A good voice coach can show you ways to vary your tone so your speech sounds more musical and attractive.

 Tone work out

1   Hum lightly and continuously.

2   Place your hand gently around your neck – as if your hand was a tie.

3   Feel all the muscles in your neck and under your jaw relax.

4   Say 'umm-hmm' in your natural speaking voice. You should feel a vibration in your face and under your hand on your neck. Feel how easily the 'hmm' part of umm-hmm comes out.

5   Now, speak with that same easy hum in your voice. Keep the sense of an easy hum in the front of your face. Don't push. Let your speaking voice grow out of that easy hum. If you lose the hum, you lose your breath connection.

6   Relax your upper body, including your shoulders, neck and abdominal muscles, and your voice will sound gentler and more pleasant.

Pace

Fast-talking used car sales people, politicians and lawyers shoot out their words like bullets. Slow talkers drag them out so you end up hanging on their words. Both types of speakers attempt to use speed to exert control over their listeners and hopefully increase their impact.

Normal conversational speech occurs in rapid bursts of sound, which is why talking more slowly can often be so effective in building your Charisma Effect. Ways to slow down include:

- add more pauses to give people time to think
- vary your delivery pace, so sometimes you slow down and at other times speed up
- use less energy in actually speaking, so words come out more smoothly and less jerkily.

If you think you talk too slowly, first check this out with colleagues since it could in fact be a great asset.

Ways to speed up your speech include:

- put more energy into actually talking so the words come out more explosively
- use verbal exercises to limber up before talking – professional actors and presenters nearly always do this as part of their preparation
- read aloud a list of some kind and time yourself with a stop watch. Practise until you read the list at faster and faster speeds.

Use silence appropriately

Those who generate a strong Charisma Effect soon realize they can use silence in a positive way by leaving leave space for reflection and for others to fill in the gaps. As US humourist Josh Billings put it: 'Silence is one of the hardest arguments to refute.'

Silence can create a feeling of openness and spaciousness for yourself and others. It can also add gravitas to how you come

silence can create a feeling of openness and spaciousness

across. You allow people time to think when you do not rush to fill silences left by others, and offer them a silent form of respect.

An entirely different kind of silence can damage your Charisma Effect by making you appear aggressive, unresponsive or simply unfriendly. Can you think of a time when you used silence as a weapon – perhaps after an argument with a friend or loved one? Once you become aware of what you are doing it becomes easier to tackle it. Gradually, as you become more vigilant the pattern will weaken. So work on the following.

- Become aware of your own silence.
- Sharpen your awareness of your own reaction to silence.
- Work at becoming comfortable with silence.
- Use silence in a positive, not negative, way.

 Silence work out

1   Phone a friend and say you want to do an experiment.

2   Explain you are both going to look at your watches and stay silent for a full 15 seconds. Try it. You both know what the plan is and yet you will be surprised at how hard it is to stay silent.

3   Next, try the same thing face to face, this time for a whole minute. What were your feelings about the experience? When did you begin to feel uncomfortable? What were the signs of discomfort? Were you able to look at the other person during the silence or did you find yourself avoiding their gaze after a while? Did you smile, laugh or make nervous noises during the silence test?

4   Try giving yourself permission to use silence for a specific purpose – for example, to make an impact in a conversation or to get feedback.

When you use silence well, you will tend to be more observant and focused. Positive silence means your mind does not function like a high-rev motor, remaining instead quiet and still. Those around you soon absorb this calmness and respond.

Silence also works well in silencing others. For example, if someone keeps chattering at you, leaving you little or no air time, you can use silence to bring this to a natural and painless end. You simply withhold encouragement through lack of positive responses such as nods, facial expressions and other kinds of verbal reinforcement. Faced with such a blank canvas the average person tends to stop talking, falling silent themselves within about two minutes.

Managers able to sit comfortably with silence in a positive way build their personal impact and make space for others to talk. They can draw out information that otherwise would not become known – for example, confronting a poorly performing member of staff or one accused of a misdemeanour.

When you use silence well you gain the power of the pause. A pause in the right place at the right time gives you time to breathe, time to consider what it is you're going to say next, time to receive and digest the feedback you're getting from your audience.

Leaders who communicate well usually listen hard for the silences of the people they are addressing. They detect enthusiastic agreement, bitter resistance or unspoken misgivings. This comes from focusing, really listening and staying present (see Chapter 4). When this happens, the leader can often achieve a strong Charisma Effect, often without saying anything at all.

'Somebody's boring me. I think it's me.'

Dylan Thomas, poet, author and playwright

Chapter 3

Confidence

*I*f you don't think you're wonderful, why should anyone else?' asked the wisecracking actress Mae West. Her legendary self-assurance did not just happen, she really worked at it.

Anthony Howard, one of Britain's most distinguished and best-known political observers, regularly appears on television. He has a famously unusual, some would say ugly, face yet his confidence soon makes you forget his looks; as he talks, his personal impact soon becomes apparent.

Self-confidence plays a vital role in creating the Charisma Effect and 'is the first requisite to great undertakings' argued Samuel Johnson, one of England's most brilliant yet notoriously ugly individuals.

> self-confidence plays a vital role in creating the Charisma Effect

Confidence conveys power; power to influence and affect people's thoughts, feelings and behaviour. Exude it and you will be more likely to make the kind of impact you want than if people see a lack of self-assurance.

Broadly, confidence means you feel sure of yourself in certain situations, but not necessarily all. It has particular relevance to interpersonal communication where it directly affects the strength and impact of your verbal and non-verbal behaviour.

Even Winston Churchill was not always entirely sure of himself and complained bitterly to his wife Clementine that, despite being prime minister, he felt inadequate and without a strong impact when dealing with important people and particular actors on the world stage. In his case, he was such a powerful figure that his Charisma Effect and his audiences' expectations helped disguise his occasional lapses in confidence.

Occasionally there is a difference between the internal confidence you possess and the external confidence you convey to others. For example, even the best stage actors may admit to internal doubts and lack of self-assurance when tackling important roles, yet once they appear on stage you would never know they are so uncertain.

But more often there is a strong link between internal confidence and the external results other people interpret as self-assurance. As one commentator puts it: 'If you think you have confidence you do, and if don't think you have got it, even if you have it, you don't have it.'

Sustained confidence arises through practise, leading to some new ability (competence), which in turn results in being more sure of yourself (confidence):

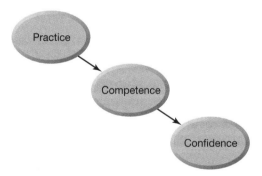

Confident behaviour shows itself in posture and other less obvious aspects of your behaviour, such as subtle body language signals. For example, other people experience you as:

- being relaxed, rather than rigid
- being flexible, with a wide-ranging voice and movement
- being in control – your movements are not shaky or awkward
- having a clear intention.

You can practise all of these – for example, getting clearer about your intention or becoming more aware about your body language. Also check out Chapter 8 on demeanour.

Try these ways to deliberately convey confidence to others.

- Intent: develop a strong, clear intention about the effect you want to achieve and stay fully conscious of it.
- Relax: create an open body posture suggesting you are ready for anything.
- Voice: cultivate a pleasant voice with variations that also conveys assuredness.
- Open-ended questions: use these to involve other people and avoid the more limited yes or no answer; then follow these up with appropriate comments and more questions.
- You-statements: these directly address the other person – not in an accusatory way but one that signals a direct and personalized focus on the other person – for example, 'Do you agree?', 'How do you feel about that?'
- Avoid powerless language: steer clear of statements that express a lack of conviction, make you sound like a victim (see Chapter 1) or seem unduly self-critical.
- Be proactive: take the initiative in the conversation process; introduce issues or views that allow others to make a contribution.
- Look people in the eye and maintain eye contact long enough to send a clear message: 'I am confident, I am interested in you.'

These are simple techniques, yet with practice they not only send a message of confidence, they also build your actual confidence.

Act as if

By the simple act of assuming you already possess confidence you can actually reduce fears and doubts that may churn through your mind in so many situations such as entering a room full of strangers, giving a talk or arguing your case in a team meeting.

act as if people want
to hear what you have
to say

Behave as if others are happy to see you and they are more likely to feel that way. Act as if people want to hear what you have to say and they will tend to do so. Act as if they respect you and they are more willing to treat you accordingly. Eventually it no longer becomes an act.

The 'act as if' principle requires you to invest most of your attention on the other person, or members of the group. Rather than wasting energy dealing with internal self-doubt you simply refuse to give it house room.

By focusing on what is happening outside of yourself you will tend to generate more confidence in yourself and others. As you increase your external focus the less self-conscious you will tend to be. With repetition it will become more natural and evolve into an unconscious pattern of behaviour.

Behave like a victim and, sure enough, that is how people will experience you. Assume people will ignore you, then that is exactly what will happen. With the Charisma Effect it always comes down to a choice – 'How am I going to be?'

● **People will assume about you, what you assume about yourself:** Your attitudes bounce back to you from other people. For example, if you think members of your team will probably ignore you, eventually the team will agree with you. If you think you have no opinions, then people will start seeing you as someone with nothing to say. Think of yourself as charming, intelligent and someone of substance, and sure enough that is how eventually you will be perceived.

● **People will tend to mirror back your present emotional state**: If you are enthusiastic others will tend to become enthusiastic too; if you are unhappy about being in the room with people, they will feel that way about you too; if you are interested about people, they will tend to be interested about you.

● **Expectations about how people will behave affect their actual behaviour**: If you think your boss hates you, chances are they will end up doing just that; if you do not expect people to sit up and take notice when you arrive, they will get the message and respond accordingly.

How does this self-fulfilling process work? Are people reading your mind, or what? To some extent they do just that, but not using telepathy. Instead they read the many deliberate and hidden messages given out through your bearing, your facial expression, your gestures and other body language. When you 'act as if', you cannot help sending out the positive messages that make an impact.

Scenarios and affirmations

These mental gymnastics can also influence how you approach communication challenges, from speaking at conferences to entering a room full of strangers, from meeting your boss to raising an issue in a team meeting. You imagine a whole experience to suit the occasion. Here are three different scenarios.

1 **You are a party host**: You pretend everyone you encounter in an event is a guest at your party, paying particular attention to each person before moving on to the next. This is a great confidence builder because you certainly have the right to be at your own party!

2 **Curiosity**: You give yourself a target to focus on, such as being curious about why people have chosen to attend a meeting. Equally, you could choose to be curious about their views on some issue or if they have blue eyes. It hardly matters, so long as you give yourself a curiosity target to work on. This externalizes your thoughts and establishes communication.

3 **Message giver:** You approach every encounter as creating a unique opportunity to convey your important message. You talk to people as if they are keen to hear your message.

Affirmations provide a continuous stream of mental reassurance, a way of strengthening your confidence. Each affirmation describes the world as *if* it is already like you want it to be. For example:

● 'I am a really interesting person.'

● 'People are desperate to hear what I will say.'

● 'This presentation is a stunning success.'

● 'I am fluent and quick thinking.'

● 'My opinions really matter.'

Invent any affirmation you want, so long as it is something in which you can believe and can keep remembering. Throughout the day, or on your way to an encounter, constantly repeat the affirmation in your mind, like a meditational mantra. Eventually you start behaving as if it is true, and in turn this affects how you behave with other people.

Emotional intelligence

Emotional intelligence (or EI) is being aware about what is happening to others emotionally and at the same time knowing how your own emotions are affected. For example, low emotional intelligence would be not realizing that you make others feel devalued, inadequate, intimidated, angry, frustrated or guilty.

While there is some debate about how far one can increase ordinary intelligence, you can certainly develop your emotional intelligence. What sets emotional intelligence apart from ordinary people skills is the ability to read the social dynamic – or what is happening at any moment during an interaction (see Chapter 12).

Developing your emotional intelligence means you also become socially aware and this can generate personal magnetism. Having a magnetic personality is therefore potentially within the reach of all of us. You attract people because they experience you as intensely aware of them – in showbiz terms, it is the audience that counts, not oneself.

Emotional intelligence is like a special radar for reading situations and interpreting the behaviours of others, their intentions, emotional states and willingness to interact. The trouble is, we sometimes suffer from radar blind spots where we either misread a situation or do not read it at all. For example, if you feel free to walk over to someone and immediately launch into saying how terrific your company is, regardless of whether they are ready to hear about it, then you have failed to read the radar correctly. Or if you say something that completely upsets another person and do not even realize it, then again your radar has failed.

> emotional intelligence is like a special radar

Ways to increase your emotional intelligence

Other chapters deal with aspects of improving your emotional intelligence, in particular those on aim (Chapter 1) authenticity (Chapter 5), presence (Chapter 4) and rapport (Chapter 12). Here we will focus on situational awareness, being able to 'read' the situational radar screen.

Useful tools to help you read the situation include the following.

- Space – what is the spatial picture in this situation?
- Behaviours – what do you observe in this situation?
- Advanced sensory activity – what is happening in this situation?
- Words and symbols – what are the signs of thought and meaning in this situation?

Space

Human beings inhabit a space and you can read a lot from how they choose to do that. For example, when you attend your next meeting, as you enter, look around at how people have chosen to spread themselves out, or not, whether they are leaning inwards or outwards, and what other signals you can pick up from the spatial picture before you.

Does the spatial arrangement seem businesslike, tranquil, alert, strained or part of a ritual? Do people look comfortable or ill at ease? Does the picture seem welcoming or not? Who sits where and why – for example, does the most senior person always sit at the head of the table. Where would it be best to place yourself in this picture and why?

Next time you enter someone's office, take a closer look at the spatial arrangements. Do they seem designed to emphasize the occupant's power? Do they promote or deter communication, or encourage or discourage any intimacy? What else can you read from the spatial arrangements?

Behaviours

When you apply emotional intelligence you observe closely other people's behaviour and consciously look for non-verbal information about the situation, including body postures, movements, gestures, facial expressions, pitch and tone of voice. These behaviours can signal all sorts of messages that once spotted you must then try to make sense of. For example, how do people in the room signal deference or authority, who touches whom, or enters the room first or last?

Try watching the TV or a film with the sound off and observe how people move and communicate without words. This kind of observation is what experienced poker players often rely on to 'read' their opponents.

Advanced sensory activity – what is happening?

This goes beyond overt behaviours and involves being alert to far less obvious factors that may tell you how people are feeling and what they are thinking. For example, watch people's breathing – are they taking shallow or deep breaths, breathing rapidly or apparently calmly?

Check out involuntary signs such as the pallor of people's skin. What is this telling you about what is happening inside the person. For example, if someone looks flushed is it a signal of disagreement, anger or perhaps embarrassment?

> check out involuntary signs such as the pallor of people's skin

Finally, assess people's energy levels – are they high or low, rising or falling? Signs of changing energy levels may stem from many sources such as body posture, eye contact, hand or foot movements and so on.

Words and symbols

This final tool is about paying close attention to the words and symbols that show up on your social radar. Since words and symbols can have such different meanings to each of us it is a miracle that we communicate at all.

To bring this issue to life, choose someone you admire and describe them to a friend. No matter how many words you use, you cannot entirely communicate your experience so your friend knows this person in the same way. Their mental picture of the person will only be a vague version of the one you know.

Even single words can have different meanings to each person. If you say you are passionate about injustice, I may assume you belong to Amnesty International, when in fact you may be referring to poverty and the impact of climate change on developing countries.

Practise watching people to see how they show their status through their language, slang, figures of speech, use or avoidance of swearing, or use of specialized vocabulary such as jargon.

'If you think you can, you can. If you think you can't, you're right.'

Mary Kay Ash, successful business woman who created one of the Fortune 100 best companies to work for, and best-selling author

Chapter 4

Presence

I n the seminal film *All That Jazz*, the main character starts his day each morning by staring intensely at his image in the mirror before urging, 'It's show time!' He is intensely aware that from the moment he leaves the quiet of his home he is permanently 'on stage'. While you may not need to remind yourself daily that it's show time, you

> you do need to evolve your own way of switching on your alertness

do need to evolve your own way of switching on your alertness for those moments where being fully present really matters.

Once there was an extraordinary woman who could not see, hear or speak well enough to be understood by most people. Her remaining senses were surprisingly average. Despite these limitations, she wrote best-selling books, appeared in vaudeville, took Hollywood by storm and won an Oscar, toured the world lecturing, and met many world figures. Countless people fell under her spell, many sobbing uncontrollably in her presence.

Such was Helen Keller's power that for many years she was one of the most famous people in the world. Her Charisma Effect was certainly at the extreme end of the spectrum we described in Chapter 1. Strangely, Helen often wrote or talked of her 'seeing' or 'hearing'. Of course, she could not literally hear noises, experiencing them instead through other ways, from subtle vibrations, air currents, aromas and textures. She always knew intimately what was happening around her. Using her remaining senses she learned to become fully present in the moment.

The transforming power of presence explains why the extreme version of the Charisma Effect can seem so awesome and even unattainable. Yet it is also incredibly familiar. Presence is intimacy, it is what allows human beings to survive, it occurs when across a crowded room your eyes meet another's and a spark flares. With presence you encounter someone else, they know you and you know them – and somehow you are both changed.

Nor is this presence solely restricted to humanity. Some years ago I sat on the grass outside a circle of fences watching a horse whisperer making contact with a beautiful young stallion. She had learned to be utterly present and the horse felt it and responded. It started doing what she wanted, not through fear but from respect, curiosity and a sense of equality.

Being fully present is an essential component of the Charisma Effect, and yet it does not have to be the extreme kind that tames horses or commands a West End stage. Take, for example, an experienced IT recruitment consultant who in a small group of strangers chats without inhibition, smiling warmly at each person, making excellent eye contact. Faintly rebuffed by one person, he moves on without resentment to the next, soon becoming the life and soul of the group. When everyone goes their separate ways most, if not all, will remember him with amusement and pleasure.

This IT recruitment consultant mobilizes his Charisma Effect, even if it is not as high octane as say Helen Keller's or other high-profile exponents of this art. His natural presence is always available when needed, and he is entirely at home with himself, knowing who he is and what really matters to him.

Presence explains many successes on the conference platform or in more informal and casual settings. In your journey towards a stronger Charisma Effect, explore your relationship to presence and therefore raise your self-awareness still further.

On our regular presentation courses, incidentally called Performing With Presence, participants experiment with feeling what it is like to be fully present. We do not attempt a Helen Keller moment by asking them to simultaneously shut their eyes and block their ears. Instead, we invite them to pause, relax in their chairs and to look around, contemplating what they can detect using their focused senses. Many express surprise at what they discover.

Try it for yourself, using the work out below as a guide.

Presence work out

1 Sit fully upright in your chair, alert, relaxed and looking forward.

2 Become aware of your breathing – focus on your body moving the air in and out, in and out.

3 Slow your breath down slightly by pausing five seconds on an intake of air, then let go and push the air out as if sending it down to your feet. Do this at least five times.

4 Without moving your head or eyes, start noticing what reaches your peripheral vision – the outside edges of your sight.

5 Pay close attention to the sounds around you. Listen for what seems near and far, loud and soft, high and low, regular or sporadic.

6 Sniff the air gently three or four times. What does the air taste like, are there are particular smells you notice? If you are wearing perfume or aftershave, try to detect it.

7 Moving your attention to your body, try to become aware of the sensation caused by your socks or footwear. Can you feel the weight of your body pressing down into the chair?

8 Experience fully this moment when life seems to slow down, and immediate pressures recede to create a new awareness.

9 Finally, start letting go of the intensity of being present, relaxing into a more familiar state of being.

At its simplest, when you are fully present you become intensely alert to your surroundings, acutely conscious of atmosphere, hidden tensions, expectations, even sometimes what people are thinking. It is worth pausing at this point to ask where did your presence go? What stops you always being present, and why is it apparently so rare to be like that?

People lose presence through being too much in the world, crowded into urban spaces and losing connection with both nature and themselves. They lose their presence through suffering some kind of emotional or other pain. And most of all they lose it by allowing their natural energies to be sapped by factors like dispiriting surroundings, unpleasant bosses, boring work, a conflict between their values and those of the organization and so on.

> people lose presence through being too much in the world

Ways to increase your presence include: reconnecting with the world; the presence highway code; using two kinds of energy; being spirited; raising your self-awareness.

Reconnecting with the world

Reconnection happens with any activity that helps to centre you – that is when you can let go of tensions, daily annoyances and distractions. It may stem from listening to a concert, walking alone on a beach at sunset, enjoying nature, meditation, singing in a choir, staring into a real log fire for hours or total involvement with a small baby.

When you reconnect, you summon back your presence, getting in touch with the essential energy that comes from within, and which also comes from without. Every human being has the ability to do this; there is no one best way for everyone. It is a journey, not a destination; you decide whether to go on it, or not.

You are being fully present when you feel at ease with yourself, entirely alive and fully alert. You notice details about how others are being and feeling, their moods and anxieties. You are curious about new ideas without being instantly judgemental, acknowledging the feelings of others. You exercise a greater intensity of hearing, smell and touch, and above all you feel energized.

The presence highway code

Mark Twain, the US humorist and author, once started a lecture by silently contemplating his audience for a prolonged period. He casually studied the auditorium as if wanting to look at every person in the eye. After nearly 10 minutes of extraordinary silence, the entire audience spontaneously broke into applause.

Twain was using an extreme version of the speaker's highway code: stop, breathe, look, listen, feel. He was getting fully in touch with his audience, making contact at a deep level and being utterly present.

The presence highway code

Stop: slow down, do not rush to start speaking. The pause gives precious moments 'to arrive' both mentally and emotionally. If you're anxious, it allows your body time to adjust and for those butterflies in your stomach to start flying in formation.

Breathe: gently take a few deep breaths, without heaving your chest or raising your shoulders. At the top of your intake of breath, hold it and count slowly to five. Doing this several times will slow your heartbeat, reducing the discharge of adrenalin into your system that causes feelings of anxiety or excitement.

▶

Look: in a small group make eye contact with each person, just briefly, before starting to talk. The effect of silence and demanding visual connection can be amazing and convey unmistakeable presence. In a large group, look for a familiar or friendly face. Continue making eye contact with a few chosen individuals across the entire audience.

While looking, ask yourself, 'What do I observe right now?' and hear the answers in your head as you continue without speaking.

For example, you may notice people smiling, frowning, looking distracted, fiddling with phones or shuffling papers. What is this telling you about the state of readiness of your audience?

Listen: for sounds that convey something useful about the people with whom you are about to communicate. Are they restless or is there a stillness suggesting they are ready for you to begin?

Feel: use all your senses, including your natural intuition, to detect what is happening around you. Give all senses full rein to uncover subtle signs that might suggest how best to communicate at this moment.

Use two kinds of energy

Watch someone with an obvious presence and even when sitting entirely still they appear energized. They are drawing upon two separate sources of power. The first stems from physicality, the alertness of the entire body for whatever will happen next, drawing energy from the outside world. The other energy used comes from within. You can tap this source of power through bringing your whole person to the situation – who you are, your values and knowing yourself. Though this sounds mystical or metaphysical, in fact you are permitting the mask to drop, so people see the individual behind it.

Here are some practical ways to draw on the energy within you.

- Give yourself permission to feel and be vulnerable. Rather than fighting tension or anxiety, tell yourself it is safe to open yourself to this person or these people.

- Think of being in a castle, lowering the drawbridge and stepping out with a gesture of welcome.

- Consciously slow down your rate of breathing (see the presence highway code earlier).

- Rather than just glancing at people, put definite energy into making eye contact, and into your facial expressions and body language. In making connections you do not do anything violent or jerky, merely act more deliberately.

- Remind yourself of your personal values and their relationship to the particular moment. If you are unsure what your personal values are, try the values work out below.

 Values work out

Becoming clear about what your personal values are can help to raise your self-awareness, feed your inner expression of energy and strengthen your presence.

1   List what you value or what matters most in your life. What do you feel really passionate about? Take time to think about this.

....

....

....

....

2   Think about how you put values into action in your life.

3   Suggest ways in which these values show up in your daily existence.

....

....

....

....

4   Choose one personal value you feel most strongly about. Would people you know well know this about you?

Show the results to a close friend or family member. Do they recognize you from seeing what you have produced? How do these values affect you at work?

Example

1   What do I value most; what am I passionate about?

The environment, justice, my marriage, being creative, my health.

2   How do I put these values into action in my daily life?

Cycle to work; active in local conservation groups; belong to Amnesty International, maintain a good work/life balance; always trying out new ideas; work out weekly; vegetarian.

Energized people with a clear positive message can create a strong presence and be extremely persuasive. Somehow, anything seems possible and all obstacles appear to be surmountable.

Be spirited

You sometimes see the lack of spirit on the football pitch, in tennis matches and other competitive situations. Heads droop, bodies flag, despondency prevails and it is not always due to running out of energy. Sometimes it is just a lack of any will to continue.

Spirited people can be magnetic; others usually like being with them because their presence vibrates with life. To experience you as spirited, people need to see you as lively, positive and animated. Smiling, laughing, expressing optimism, eyes wide and alert, body posture all contribute to conveying spirit.

Part of being spirited arises from your use of energy. Actors, for example, despite feeling low or even demoralized, learn to draw on reserves of energy to lift their spirits just before they go on

> part of being spirited arises from your use of energy

stage. You may need to do the same by paying special attention to whether or not you are fully using your energy.

Raise your self-awareness

This theme runs throughout the journey towards enhancing your Charisma Effect. Ways to deliberately increase your self-awareness include exploring the self that you hide from people, listening and trusting your intuition and connecting with people who inspire you.

Self-awareness includes discovering how your own behaviour may be actually reducing your Charisma Effect.

Explore your hidden aspects

What really lies behind your mask? If you seldom take a long look, it can be challenging to explore the hidden and perhaps uncomfortable parts of yourself. Why bother? Surely if you have tucked away part of yourself it must be for a good reason? That may be true, but if these hidden parts either reduce your Charisma Effect or could be used to enhance it, then exploring them could be extremely worthwhile.

'Well, what is my hidden self?' you may ask. While of course only you can answer that, otherwise it wouldn't be hidden, it is most likely to consist of some of those elements listed in the hidden self work out, shown overleaf.

When you try to establish a presence, what happens? For example, do you find yourself trying to be like a movie star with exaggerated gestures or self-important types of behaviour?

Hidden self work out

1   Find a quiet place where you will not be disturbed. Put a notepad and pen beside you.

2   Using the list of headings below to stimulate your thinking, see if you can produce one or more examples about yourself and your life.

- Irrational or absurd fears
- Strong dislikes or hatreds
- Loves and passions
- Unmet needs
- Hidden or unused talents
- Seldom expressed thoughts and feelings

- Past behaviour you are proud of that you rarely or never talk about
- Behaviour you feel bad about and seldom if ever think about
- Revealing stories or incidents
- Seldom expressed desires and wishes

3   What does your list suggest about you? Is there anything on it that might be directly influencing how you behave when with other people, either positively or negatively?

Listen and trust your intuition

The Arctic Tern is a bird that lives seven degrees south of the North Pole and once a year flies 23,000 incredible miles back to its starting point. With a homing instinct like that it needs no fancy SatNav. Its instinct tells it where to go and how to get there. Humans too have an inbuilt ability to find our way through life and to home in on what is happening around us. Think of it as a radar, not something you can fit on a spreadsheet.

A small village in central Europe invited a rabbi famous for his wisdom to visit them. For weeks the local Jewish population debated what issues to raise with him, what conflicts they wanted resolved, what advice to ask for. Finally the rabbi arrived and everyone gathered to welcome him. He stood silent, becoming fully present, taking in his surroundings, sensing the atmosphere. Instead of speaking he began to dance. He danced and danced and soon everyone was doing the same. When everyone had danced themselves to a standstill, in the panting silence that followed, the rabbi quietly asked: 'Any more questions?'

According to doctor of psychology Professor Cappon, who writes and researches the subject, intuition is the 'jewel in the crown of intelligence'. Compared to conscious reasoning, he argues that intuition is 'the secret of success in most human endeavours'.

Despite its apparent importance, though, not much about intuition surfaces in books or articles on communication or its role in building presence. This mainly reflects the assumption that it involves soft data and is therefore unreliable. Yet there is nothing irrational about intuition, even when it happens to be wrong. Some believe that we base 90% of the decisions we make on intuition.

One accepted view of intuition is that at some hidden level you already know the answer and instinct merely lets you access it. For example, knowing someone is lying may not come directly from hearing their words, but from subtle physiological changes they cannot control but which give the game away. You may not even know you are recording these signs, yet unconsciously you are. By trusting your instinct, you allow this knowledge to surface.

While negotiating to buy the Atkins Computer Group in the UK, Jack Roseman, founder of two successful computer firms and president of a third said: 'I can't tell you precisely what it was that told me within seconds that our only hope of acquiring the company was to win the hearts and minds of the managers sitting around the table.'

Asked by the owner whether he would like to see the accounts, Roseman used his intuition to respond that he wanted everyone to get to know each other first. If the chemistry was wrong, 'you could give me this company for nothing and I wouldn't want it'.

This was exactly what people wanted to hear, and he won the deal, despite offering less money than his competitor.

There are many ways you might apply intuition when building your presence. Even when you have few hard facts to go on you might use:

- foresight – anticipating an event
- hindsight – understanding what caused something to happen
- hunch – the initial and likely answer to a problem
- knowing – being sure you know the best ways to reach a solution or use a discovery, or the best time to intervene or the significance of something.

You can sharpen and hone your intuition through practice and experimentation (see the following work outs below).

 Intuition work out

1 Set aside some specific times when you intend to explore your intuition – these could be when you are alone or, better still, when you are in a situation where you want to make a personal impact.

2 Use real issues and problems, not theoretical ones, to explore intuition. It works best in live situations rather than on meaningless tasks.

3 Allow yourself to examine what you are feeling and try to note how it is affecting you at that moment. For example, 'I feel tired right now and notice I'm getting increasingly impatient.'

4 Acknowledge or accept these feelings, even when uncomfortable. For example, 'I accept I'm angry right now and it's understandable I'm impatient.'

5 Treat your intuition as a quiet, respectful friend who usually waits to be asked for an opinion. Invite your intuition to give you a response. For example, 'I accept I am angry right now. What does this mean I should do next?'

6 Check your intuition's accuracy and your response to it.

Additional intuition work out

1 **Diary**: Keep an intuition diary where you record impressions, whether they stem from dreams, sensations or instant thoughts. Examine these to see what insights they offer about your intuition – for example, when it seems to work best or in what environment.

2 **Interests**: Use your hobbies or interests to explore your intuition. Musicians have intuitions about music, scientists about science, parents about children, professionals about their particular subject.

3 **Answers**: Pick a problem or issue to which you want answers. Take a walk in green spaces and while enjoying your surroundings pick up an object such as a stone, a leaf or whatever is lying there. Look closely at it and ask your natural intuition: 'What insights can this give me about my question?'

Hints

● Treat with suspicion intuition that seems to be commanding you to do something, rather than suggesting possibilities.

● Combine your intuition with your logic.

● If you have an intuition, treat this with respect, as if it is advice given by a trusted colleague.

Preparing the body

As part of your preparation work to communicate your message, you may need to wake up your whole being, especially if you are giving a stand-up, formal presentation.

Tension before a live performance is perfectly natural; it is a form of concentrated energy to be properly harnessed. For example, before an important

> tension before a live performance is perfectly natural

performance, actors spend an hour or more preparing their bodies. They work hard to unwind, relax and get themselves ready to communicate. Whenever you intend to achieve a strong Charisma Effect, you can usefully do this kind of preparation too. Using physical work you start taking control of the impact you want to make.

Particularly if you are giving a formal presentation, your body preparation work needs to be thorough and may consist of the following.

- Physical relaxation exercises: shake separate parts of your body to remove tension; close your eyes and focus on each part of the body in turn checking for tension; breathe deeply in and out slowly, while telling that part to let go and relax.

- Voice exercises to loosen up the throat and vocal chords: hum gently, make simple sounds such as aahhs and oos; say out loud a tongue twister, such as 'Red Leather, Yellow Leather, Red Leather, Yellow Leather', to help loosen your speech muscles.

- Stay away from smokers and avoid shouting or lengthy talking.

Physical warm-ups wake up your mind, body, breath and voice; they help make you fully ready to achieve your aim.

'Just being present emotionally in the scene, truly present emotionally, should be enough to convey what should be conveyed.'

Lasse Hallström, Swedish film director

Chapter 5

Authenticity

The legendary conductor, composer, and pianist Leonard Bernstein was once asked by a photographer to pose for a picture inside an airport while sitting on a motorcycle. 'I don't ride a motorcycle,' Bernstein protested, 'it would be phony.' 'I'm sure you could ride it if you tried', the photographer replied.

To the amazement of his colleagues Bernstein jumped aboard, shot off at top speed across the airfield, slowed briefly to demonstrate a few tricky manoeuvres and returned to the shoot. 'Now,' he proclaimed, 'you can take your picture.'

We live in a world seemingly accelerating in the opposite direction to being authentic. Globalization, lifestyle technology, spin doctors, advertising, virtual goods and services, online communities, even electronic lovers. They all conspire to undermine what is real or lasting, including human relationships.

A formula for how to be authentic would not be real. When someone is authentic they simply come across as themselves and not anyone else – there is no rule for how they do it. Quite simply, what you see is what you get. Everyone is born authentic. You don't see babies trying to be anyone but themselves. Starting in childhood and moving through adolescence and into adulthood, though, our spontaneity is knocked out of us, until we end up asking 'Who am I, really?'

> a formula for how to be authentic would not be real

This separation becomes second nature. As adults, we may be reluctant or unable to remove the mask so people can see who we really are, directly affecting the impression we make on them. For example, Lord Reith, the first BBC chairman was a hard-to-know person who had severe mood swings. At his daughter's wedding reception, her psychiatrist husband was told by a guest, 'I'd really like to meet Lord Reith.' To which the husband replied, 'So would I.'

As writer Marianne Williamson put it memorably: 'Our deepest fear is that we are powerful beyond measure. It is our light, not our darkness, that most frightens us. We ask ourselves, who am I to be brilliant, gorgeous, talented, fabulous? Actually, who are you not to be?'[1]

Authenticity underpins a strong Charisma Effect and proves particularly important if you happen to manage or lead people. But you cannot declare yourself to be authentic, it is up to other people to decide that you are.

Others first need to see you are true to yourself, know who you are and use that to communicate what you want. Former HR director of Marks & Spencer, Jean Tomlin, reportedly explained: 'I want to be me, but I am channelling parts of me to context. What you get is a segment of me. It is not a fabrication or a fake – just the bits that are relevant for that situation.'

Authenticity works through people identifying with you at a personal, human level. Putting it slightly differently, they feel connected in some way with who you are and what you stand for. To be authentic, people must hear your distinctive voice and experience those qualities that are unique to you.

Authentic performance on a personal level is the ability to express who you are, while being fully aware of the influence you are having around you. It is an act of dual attention. First you need self-awareness and, secondly, a sensitivity to the effect on your audience. This contributes to the chemistry we discuss later. It leads to an impactful first impression, a lasting impression and a sustainable relationship.

[1] Often wrongly attributed to Nelson Mandela.

Being authentic produces benefits far beyond simply improving communications, teambuilding or promoting the brand. By removing the mask, people and indeed entire companies can become who they really are, knowing their purpose and their values. 'I couldn't be out of character, I just had to be myself', commented the larger than life Karen Darby on not being selected as one of the dragon judges on the TV series *Dragon's Den* that aims to find budding entrepreneurs.

When you meet someone who is not being authentic or true to themselves you soon sense something is wrong. Sometimes we say 'he was putting on act' or 'she is not entirely reliable'. Try the authenticity work out to stimulate your thinking about what makes you authentic.

 Authenticity work out

1 Think of three or four people you have met, read about or heard of who you admire a great deal. They might be alive or dead, from your own time or some time in history.

2 Narrow the names down to just one.

3 Write the person's name in the space below and then list what you most admire about them.

I really admire ....

What I most admire about this person is
(be as specific as possible)

....

....

....

....

....

4 Why does this person seem to be authentic?

5 How does this person convey authenticity in your view?

6 How do you convey authenticity?

Being authentic

If you really admire someone, it is perfectly understandable to want to be like them. But that is different from slavishly copying them in every way. You cannot be them – they are who they are and you are who you are. Being inauthentic is thinking or behaving as if you are someone you are not.

The obsession with celebrity encourages a lack of authenticity, leading us to believe we should aspire to instant fame or fortune without needing to be true to ourselves. For example, during the 1980s at the giant GE company, 'Everyone wanted to be like Jack Welch', explained Kevin Sharer, his long-term assistant and later also a CEO. Sharer learned at first hand that 'you need to be who you are, not try to emulate someone else'.

> the obsession with celebrity encourages a lack of authenticity

During our Personal Impact learning events, we hear people say things like:

- 'I feel like I'm one person at work and another at home ... and I'm no longer sure which is me.'

- 'I'm tired of trying to figure out the hidden agendas; I wonder what we could accomplish if we all just got real?'

- 'I'm very adaptable, but I'm not sure that copying my boss' leadership style is the way to go.'

- 'I really want to be me, but it just wouldn't work in that place.'

So people come to work wearing their masks and wonder why they do not have the impact they want. Those attending the workshop often express amazement that what works about them comes from within, not from outside. Slightly incredulous they ask: 'You mean I just have to be myself?' When assured that is exactly what they need to be, you can feel the sense of relief.

People who try to use authenticity to convey charisma sometimes feel that this entitles them to let themselves go, showing anger, impatience or dissatisfaction, regardless of what it does to others. In fact, a reputation for authenticity needs to be carefully managed.

Am I being authentic?

'I don't believe a word you say,' said a journalist to a famous UK politician. 'Everything about you is phoney. Even your hair which looks like a wig isn't!' How do you know when you are not being entirely authentic? There are both internal and external warning signs.

The internal signs show that you feel somehow removed from what you are saying, disconnected from what really matters to you. You know you are 'putting on a front' and that the real you is not being allowed to emerge. You hide your thoughts, try to conceal your feelings and strongly censure what you actually say.

The external signs are that you start basing your actions not on what is right, but what is convenient or easy to go along with. You are open to pressure from others to do things that, when you think about it, you know are wrong or highly questionable.

'When Cameron threw "phoney" at him in Prime Minister's Questions, it stuck like napalm', argued one commentator about the impact of these words from the Conservative opposition leader on British prime minister Gordon Brown. Despite the apparent reduction in the importance of authenticity in favour of celebrity, still one of the most damaging accusations you can make about someone is to say they are phoney.

You cannot wake up one morning and simply declare, 'Today I am going to be authentic', because being authentic is not a goal, it is a process. You constantly adapt and recognize your fallibility. It is about:

- Your desire and ability to be real, not phony or contrived. 'If you seek authenticity for authenticity's sake, you are no longer authentic', argued philosopher Jean Paul Sartre – that is, we need to seek authenticity because it really matters to us in some way.

- How you connect with people, becoming worthy of their trust.

Warning signs you are not being authentic

- You make friends only with those who have something you want and might benefit you in the future.
- You are terrific at collecting business cards and phone numbers that will help you professionally, but have few real quality friendships or relationships.
- You manipulate others to get what you want without worrying about the effect this may have on them or yourself.
- You allow others to manipulate you.
- You focus your behaviour around gaining other people's approval, regardless of how you feel about them.
- You are not true to yourself.
- You feel lonely, disrespected and non-committal in your relationships.
- At work, you feel out of place, bored, underrated, unappreciated.
- You make little progress in your personal growth or do not even care about it.
- In your leisure time, you no longer enjoy *being* yourself, or you feel uncomfortable with those you once called your friends.
- You do not fully respect yourself and do not really believe in your own personal values or follow them in terms of actions.
- Even your compliments make people feel bad. They sound genuine at first but as the truth soaks in your real intention becomes clear.

We often sum up an authentic person and their personal impact on us as: 'What you see is what you get.' Almost absurdly, the easiest way to be more authentic is ... be more like yourself!

> the easiest way to be more authentic is ... be more like yourself!

The comic George Burns once said of honesty, 'If you can fake it, you've got it made.' He could equally have been talking about authenticity. Faking authenticity, though, is much harder work than merely being yourself.

A study of over 1,000 business leaders, chosen for their authenticity and effectiveness, found they were constantly testing themselves through real-life experiences. They wanted to discover the purpose of their leadership and had learned that being authentic made them more effective.[2] Even if you are not a leader in an organization, this research finding is encouraging. It shows that being authentic is about a manageable process of constantly checking with reality, using it to determine 'Who am I?', 'What matters to me?', 'What do I want?' rather than expecting authenticity to instantly occur after intensive training or being born with an 'authentic' gene.

Style check

Your personal style affects how people experience your authenticity. For example, you may see your style as man or woman about town, cool and in control, but is that how you actually come across?

Imagine you had your own private public relations company working on your behalf or that a high-powered advertising agency was contracted to promote you to the world. One of the issues both sorts of experts would want to explore with you is:

● what is your personal brand?

[2] George, Bill, Sims, Peter Mclean, Andrew N. and Meyer, Diana (2007) 'Discovering your authentic leadership', *Harvard Business Review*, Article R0702H, 1 February 2007.

Your brand contains everything you say and do; how you look, talk, think, move and behave. It's almost as if you were a company called, say, Me PLC. What would be the Me PLC brand? Just as we recognize that John Lewis, Zara, Apple or Nokia have their own styles and branding, so too does Me PLC. The more you become aware of this brand, the more you will succeed at showing your authenticity and strengthen your Charisma Effect.

How would you describe each of these individuals' personal brands?

● Camilla
● Russia's Mr Putin
● Oprah Winfrey
● José Mourinho
● Gordon Ramsay
● Denzel Washington
● Andrew Marr.

Do they have a distinctive style, if so what makes it so? How authentic does this tend to make them in your view?

 Style work out (1)

Here are some ways to start reviewing and thinking about your personal style.

Complete the descriptions below and try to explain why you have chosen your various responses.

1 If I was a car, I would be a (e.g. a Mercedes) ....
   because (e.g. I'm about quality and style) ....

   ....

2 If I was a food, I would be a (e.g. a grapefruit) ....
   because (e.g. I am a bit sharp but good for you) ....

   ....

3 If I was a shop, I would be like (e.g. Marks & Spencer) ....
because (e.g. I give good value for what I have on offer) ....

....

● Looking at your answers, what do they suggest about your personal style?
● Would your friends or colleagues agree with your descriptions?
● How closely do you think you live the brand?
● Use the above to complete the second style work out below.

Style work out (2)

At a meeting with your personal PR company or advertising agents, these experts want to convey your authenticity to the world. First, they decide to get a better picture of your personal brand, your particular style.

How would you describe your brand to them?

For example:

My brand is more like a Toyota than a BMW. I deliver quality without making a big fuss about it and don't push my style at you. I like to be seen as a brand that delivers to the customer – that is, I get things done and you can rely on me. I am also rather like some of the better stores, in that I don't get defensive if you find something wrong with what I do, I'll simply accept I got things wrong and try to put them right. I am also a bit like First Direct bank: I am easily accessible and when you do contact me I bet you find me friendly and patient.

....

....

....

....

....

....

....

▶

Next, the consultants decide to design a logo that conveys who you are and what you stand for. What would this logo look like? Draw it, don't just describe it! Even if you cannot draw, try it all the same.

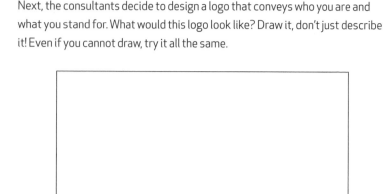

Reviewing the above, and also the results from the earlier style work out, what have you learned about your style and how you come across?

Being yourself – your values

Any large gap between how you see yourself and how others experience you can potentially reduce your ability to convey authenticity and highlight what you need to work on. So let's look more closely at this aspect of being yourself. You are being authentic when you do the following.

- **Mean what you say and say what you mean**: Being consistent in your communication with people can strengthen your impact because people come to believe what you say. For example, when you make a promise, offer a compliment, make a threat, ask for help, do you really mean it? Any serious disconnection between your words and what you really mean damages your impact:

  - 'He's all hot air.'
  - 'Her bark is worse than her bite.'
  - 'He'll promise you the earth if … .'

- 'With her it's always promises, promises.'
- 'Do you really mean that?'
- 'Thanks, but I wish I could be sure of that.'
- 'I bet it'll never happen like that.'

The better you are with words and talking the more important it is to match the words to your meaning. For example, when you are angry, happy, frustrated, busy, bored, confused, do you hide how you feel with bland phrases, platitudes and other distractions?

- **Convey you have clear principles and act on them**: What are your personal values? Do you know what you stand for and are you willing to share this with other people? Equally important, do people see you acting on what truly matters to you?

Many managers, for example, talk enthusiastically about customer care while their disillusioned staff witness them creating systems or processes that demonstrate quite the opposite. Be willing to use phrases like:

- 'What really matters to me is ... .'
- 'Here is where I stand on this ... .'
- 'I feel it is very important that ... .'
- 'I cannot go along with that because ... .'
- 'That would go against what I believe in, which is ... .'
- 'This is wrong because ... .'
- 'This is the right thing to do and I want to do it.'

- **Show you are reliable and can be depended upon**: Sure ways to signal 'you cannot depend on me' include turning up late for meetings, losing track of what people have asked you to do, agreeing to do things and then failing to deliver.

When one of my close business colleagues agrees to send me a book or some information I need, he always writes it down meticulously on his action list, carried in a folder. Once it is down on that list I know for sure it will happen without fail. In 20 years of working with him I have seldom been let down.

Being reliable and dependable is like gold plating your personal impact. Clearly one can still make a big impact even though unreliable, but this is despite such negative behaviour and not because of it.

● **Take responsibility for developing yourself to your full potential.**

● **Match your inner reality to its outward appearance.**

 ## Values work out (1)

Round 1

Write a short mission statement that explains to you the following.

1   Why you think you are on this planet.

2   What really and truly matters to you – your values.

3   What you want to do to make your life meaningful.

Round 2

1   Revise this material until you are satisfied that it expresses what your life is all about.

2   Type it out.

3   Show it to someone you like and trust and ask them to share their reaction to it with you.

Round 3

1   In the light of the comments or response you have received, revise the material again until you feel satisfied with it.

2   Print out the material in large size (16 pt or bigger).

3   Put this material on your wall or where you will see it daily.

4   Read it every day and keep asking: 'Am I living the mission I want in my life?'

Values work out (2)

1 For the next seven days, keep track of any situations where other people try to get you to do things that contradict your personal values.

2 Write down the situations and how they made you feel?

3 How did you assert your right to act authentically?

Finally it is worth devising your own guidelines for practising the craft of authentic performance. For example, you might set yourself the following principles.

● Stay awake and be present.

● Notice your own bullshit.

● Allow yourself to be challenged on any inauthentic actions.

● Seek constant and honest feedback.

● Take a personal inventory of your values.

● Express yourself.

● Talk about what's important to you, rather than chit-chat.

● Be purposeful.

● Stay in touch with what you are passionate about.

'To be nobody but yourself, in a world which is doing its best, night and day, to make you everybody else, means to fight the hardest battle which any human being can fight; and never stop fighting.'

e e cummings, US poet

Chapter 6

Courage

There was an expectant buzz from the delegates. Shortly they would hear from an expert on inspirational leadership. Finally, the speaker entered from the back of the room and to people's amazement began singing. Striding towards the conference platform still singing loudly, people responded to his lyrics and their passionate, relevant message. Once he began speaking he had already captured their attention entirely, establishing an impressive Charisma Effect.

Are you willing to take risks to build your Charisma Effect, stepping into the unknown? Or do you hate taking risks, while still wanting to improve your personal impact? If so, maybe it is time to do some self-awareness work around risk taking.

Although using interesting or challenging ways to communicate your message can definitely strengthen your Charisma Effect, being reckless could undermine it. For example, when meeting a new client you might risk making your point by reading a poem, showing a cartoon or even doing a magic trick. But, of course, to make the point by plunging a six-inch kitchen knife into the conference table would almost certainly appear reckless and do little to enhance your positive impact.

Courage is also not necessarily about dramatic risk taking – it can be as simple as daring to use your physicality more actively to get yourself across to

> courage is also not
> necessarily about
> dramatic risk taking

people. If you are naturally expressive with your hands, face and body then courage may not be an issue, but for many people, deliberately being more expressive using their physical being can certainly seem to demand courage.

To develop courage in your interpersonal communications you need both regular practise and plenty of feedback. If necessary, make sure you ask for it.

Intelligent risk taking

It is worth taking risks that help get your message across when you have weighed up whether:

● the benefits would outweigh the costs if it all goes wrong

● there is only a remote chance of the worst case situation actually happening (see the upside–downside box, opposite).

Also, what appears to be risky or to demand a great deal of courage, may on closer examination prove just to be a fear of shadows. Working with your fear is therefore part of developing your courage to be different. Try the fear work out below.

 Fear work out

● Find a quiet, safe place where you will not be disturbed for at least half an hour.

● Lie on the floor, feet up on a chair, with a thin cushion under your head.

● Take long, slow breaths, keeping it deep and steady.

● Start to speak your fears aloud, 'I am frightened of ...'.

● Begin with objects or animals, such as spiders, cars, computers.

● Now move on to events, such as giving a talk, entering a room full of strangers, meeting the boss privately.

● Next mention the people you feel frightened of: a parent, boss, a partner, a sibling, a colleague at work.

● Finally, say aloud the names of people or events from your past that generated fear. Do they still exist? What do you currently fear most right now – flooding, terrorism, loss of health? What do you fear in the future?

● Make sure you say the fears out loud, not safely inside your head.

During this work out you may feel tearful, anxious or find your body is tensing up and you have an urge to get up and do something entirely different. Stick with it though, since by naming your fears they begin to lose their power over you.

Upside–downside: making sense of risk taking

1   You ask a client for the order you have been diligently chasing.

● Worst case downside = client refuses; decides to end the relationship.

● Best case upside = you get the order; establish a long-lasting, profitable relationship.

2   In a one-to-one session, you demand that a colleague improves her performance.

● Worst case downside = the person gets angry; resigns claiming you are bullying or showing unfair discrimination.

● Best case upside = person thanks you for your frankness: agrees to try harder and afterwards sings your praises to others.

3   You enter a room and talk to the first person you see who is free to engage with you.

● Worst case downside = person rejects your approach rudely; walks away leaving you feeling awful.

● Best case upside = person responds with enthusiasm; you make a friend or business contact for life; it leads to a major contract.

▶

In each case, what is the chance of the worst case actually happening? If it is extremely small, then the risk may be worth taking, given the potential best case situation or some variation on it happening.

Making these kinds of mental calculations is what intelligent risk taking is about.

You need emotional resilience to handle possible unfavourable results from your risk taking. Such resilience usually only comes through experimenting and exploring the risky area.

Strangely, some people feel fine about taking physical risks, such as climbing, abseiling or whitewater rafting, while strenuously avoiding the social risks needed to get their message across with impact.

Whether you are an introvert or an extrovert may also influence your risk taking. For example, extroverts may find risk taking fun, seeing it as just part of being sociable and assertive. By contrast, introverts may find it distasteful. While you cannot easily move from being one to the other, it can help to become more aware of how your basic personality may be inhibiting or encouraging risk taking.

extroverts may find risk taking fun

Risk taking that builds your Charisma Effect may mean you:

- show the courage to challenge or question people
- have a point of view and express it
- stand up for your beliefs in the face of opposition
- accept alternative views without being defensive
- make full use of physical expression.

Let's look at these more closely.

Challenge or question people

A new CEO of an insurance company called a town hall meeting to introduce himself to all the staff. After the formal introductions, he took the risk of telling a personal story about dealing with a travel agency. He shared with everyone how the agency's outstanding customer care made him feel, how he experienced a burst of gratitude to the agency for resolving what could have been a frustrating and worrying problem. Looking around the packed room, the new CEO asked if anyone else had recently experienced exceptional customer care.

Soon people who would never normally have spoken to a chief executive in public began sharing their own stories of customer care. At just the right moment, the CEO smiled and explained his vision that people who dealt with his new company would talk to their friends in just this way about its wonderful customer care.

There was an awkward silence and at last someone ventured: 'But we always have good ratings in the annual industry measures for customer care.' The CEO nodded, 'I absolutely agree, so it's clear we have a strong platform on which to build something truly outstanding. That is what I want to do, it's an absolute commitment of mine and I want it to be yours too.'

After the meeting, people often talked at length about the new CEO and how he had come across and excited them with his vision of the future. No one mentioned charisma, but the CEO had conveyed it strongly through his challenge and questioning.

Do you feel comfortable challenging people and confronting them over things which you disagree about? People with strong personal impact usually have the courage to question the status quo, deal with conflict and ask awkward questions, even when they may alienate some people.

While challenge can be charisma enhancing, it normally needs to be constructive, rather than destructive. If you constantly complain about situations, always raise impossible to answer questions, seldom agree with people about anything or generally prove hard to work with, people will see you as offering an unwelcome kind of challenge.

Constructive challenge, on the other hand, stimulates because it can inject fresh thinking, offer alternatives to consider and engage people's interest. Nor is it always necessary to feel comfortable doing it; those on the receiving end merely need to see you are challenging in a spirit of enquiry, rather than, say, vindictiveness.

People with a strong charisma perfect ways of posing the right questions so they enliven, rather than threaten. Part of this may stem from offering challenge in a friendly manner; it may also come from not making people wrong.

An example

Destructive challenge:	'Your strategy makes no sense to me, how on earth did you arrive at it?'
Constructive challenge:	'Could you take me through your strategy so I can understand how you arrived at it?
Destructive challenge:	Our customer care is rubbish and you know it.
Constructive challenge:	Our current customer care seems to have plenty of scope for improvement; do you agree?
Destructive challenge:	Why did you mess up delivering this report on time again?
Constructive challenge:	What do you think is preventing you getting your reports in on time?

Challenge work out

Change the following challenges from destructive into constructive ones.

'You couldn't be more wrong. We just don't do it that way.'

....

'It's happening again. This team is wasting time on yet another pointless debate.'

....

'If you can find a better supplier than us let me know.'

....

'This agenda is nonsense, why don't we focus on the really important issues?'

....

'Well it may inspire you, but it doesn't inspire me.'

....

Now create three real constructive challenges for others in your life.

....

....

....

Have a point of view and express it

If you do not know where you are going, any road will do. Without a point of view you become less interesting to others and weaken your charisma. People making a strong personal impact usually have something to say for themselves, using phrases like:

- 'My view is ...'
- 'The way I see it is ...'
- 'I can't agree with that because ...'

- 'What matters to me about this is …'
- 'What I want is …'
- 'I would prefer that …'
- 'From my point of view …'

Do you sometimes find it hard to know what your opinion actually is about an issue or situation? So you sit silent in meetings, finding it difficult to take a clear position on the subject under discussion? There may be several reasons why this happens.

First, the issue or situation seems outside your knowledge or experience. Second, you may actually possess a point of view yet cannot readily access it at that moment. This leads to those frustrating times when later you realize what you could have said, but did not. A third reason arises when you have a cultural background where you are not normally expected to express an opinion, especially without being asked for it.

> if you do not know where you are going, any road will do

Whatever the reason, you can start generating your own point of view about an issue by preparing, asking questions and gaining more information, relating it to something familiar.

Preparation can often provide you with a whole range of opinions, which in the heat of the moment can otherwise seem out of reach. Try to attend a meeting, a one-to-one session or other important communication situation with something ready to say. There will often be plenty of sources to stimulate you, such as a pre-planned agenda, the topic itself, reading widely, talking to other people in advance and so on.

Asking questions will often open up a topic, stimulating you to come up with an opinion, using additional information. Ask open-ended questions to encourage people to provide more than a simple yes or no answer.

Relating the issue to something familiar can be a creative stimulus to arriving at an opinion. For example, you could use:

- your personal values
- past experience or something it reminds you of
- an existing policy or guideline
- others' strong opinions and how these make you feel
- something entirely unconnected to generate a fresh insight.

Express it

Having an opinion is not enough, you also need the courage to express it. Sometimes this means offering your opinion without being asked. At other times it may be better to wait until a suitable moment arises when people will be ready to receive it.

Once people realize you often have an opinion they will start looking forward to hearing it. Incidentally this is why you see people starting to look towards certain individuals expectantly during meetings. They know from experience that these people have views and anticipate hearing them.

Staying silent and withholding your opinion may create a useful air of mystery, but if you force people to work hard to extract your views this just limits your impact. Instead, generate your point of view, listen for a break in the flow of conversation, be brave and express it.

If everyone seems too busy talking, this could mean it is best to stay quiet. However, you could be leaving the field open to those who make the most noise, and thus never get your opinion across.

If there is no break in the conversation, try the quiet voice in the background technique. You wait until someone winds down a bit and say clearly without aggression, 'I would like to say something please.' If people ignore you, repeat it again, even if you have to talk over someone else. Go on saying, 'I would like to say something please', increasingly loudly, until at last people have to stop and listen. It takes a certain amount of courage to use this technique but it will guarantee you an attentive audience.

Watch out for the opinion trap, where you find yourself becoming dogmatic, over-assertive and excessively pushing your views, regardless of whether other people

watch out for the opinion trap

want to hear them. A version of the opinion trap awaits unwary managers or leaders. Because people constantly seek your opinions you start assuming you must always immediately pronounce on what you think is right or wrong or what should be done. This instant offering of an opinion can undermine your personal impact, unless you are being complimentary – for example, noticing something done well or congratulating someone on an achievement.

The opinion trap also occurs up when people start telling you their problems. Unwary sales people often fall into it, believing the client is actually asking for advice. In fact the person merely wants to share an issue, without being offered an immediate fix.

Develop your ability to listen with your whole attention by offering clarifying questions such as:

- 'Do other people feel the same?'
- 'How does this make you feel?'
- 'Is this something fairly recent?'
- 'Sounds awful, what does your boss think?'
- 'Have you ever had this happen before?'
- 'What do you think they want in return?'
- 'Do you look forward to that?'
- 'Can you explain that a bit more?'

Stand up for your beliefs

'My real test of courage,' says Jacqueline Gold, chief executive of the highly successful Anne Summers retail chain that sells sexy lingerie and adult toys, 'is to be in the minority on many occasions.'

Gold's Charisma Effect consists of great poise combined with her courage to stand her ground and speak her mind about what really matters to her. She is nowhere near the far end of the charisma spectrum, yet her impact remains powerful and memorable.

'You don't like my principles? I have plenty of others', joked Groucho Marx and, in reality, many people seem like that. Faced with criticism, rejection or hostility they simply crumble. Rather than risk any conflict, instead they lapse into resentful silence or, worse, disown what they have previously put forward.

Achieving a strong personal impact partly stems therefore from being willing to stand up for your views, taking the risk of facing down opposition. Unless you are also spoiling for a fight, this need not involve a heated argument. Instead, you simply assert your right to hold your view or to hold certain values and demand that others treat this with respect.

A useful way to stand up for your beliefs is to respond by showing respect for the opposition, rather than decrying it. You say things like:

- 'I hear what you say, yet I see it rather differently.'
- 'I realize you disagree, and I'd also like my views to be taken seriously.'
- 'You obviously feel strongly about this and so do I.'
- 'That is one interpretation. I have a different one.'
- 'What really matters to me is ... .'

It can feel risky standing up for your point of view, especially if no one else seems to immediately support you, but this isolation may be misleading. Once people see you standing up for your views you may begin to attract supporters.

Accept alternative views

There is something engaging about a person with a clear point of view who does not seem to push it at you, as if trying to instantly convert you to their position. Strengthen your personal impact by showing you have the courage to hear alternative views, without becoming defensive.

As outlined in Chapter 2 on fluency, try using the technique of accept and build: when a person puts forward a different view from yours, rather than disparage it you try to build on it. You may even be able to link it to your own views and strengthen your own position further.

Use physical expression

Personal impact is the total message you send to people. As we saw earlier, words usually play a relatively minor role in your communication compared to the power of non-verbal factors, including body language.

Although personal impact stems from what you say, from the inner feelings you harbour and your attitudes to people, including yourself, it is the non-verbal clues that really make a difference.

Most of us do not realize the significance of bodily cues or even associate them with courage. Yet physical expression can take courage and when you see people making a strong personal impact they seldom appear afraid to make definite and sometimes expansive gestures. This may include using their body in positive ways to convey their message, whether it is being able to remain extremely still, to laugh uproariously, to signal intense listening or to use their hands to emphasize their point.

> most of us do not realize the significance of bodily cues

As we leave childhood we tend to lose awareness of body language and may need to work at refreshing it. Actors learn early in their training to use the body to convey that they are fully present and demand attention. For example, they practise walking as if they were complete failures, then as if they owned the entire world. In our Personal Impact workshops participants enjoy walking around experiencing how it feels to be at different status levels.

 Status work out

1 Find an empty room with plenty of space to walk around.

2 From a pack of playing cards extract a set of ace to 10 in value.

3 Shuffle these cards and pick one at random.

4 This number defines your status from 1= low to 10 = very high.

5 Using this number, start walking around the room as if this is now your status in life.

6 Pick a second number and again walk around feeling what it would be like to have that status in life. Enter a room with that 'persona'.

7 Finally do it yet again and experiment with this third level of status.

- What have you learned from doing this?

- How did your body behave at the various different status levels?

- How did you feel in each case?

- What did this work out tell you about how you might enter a room next time?

Gestures play a significant part in establishing charisma as anyone who has watched someone like ex-president Clinton soon recognizes. Hand gestures, body movements to and away from people, nodding, smiling, eye movements, turning, walking all convey his persona and undoubted charm.

Next time you are in a meeting, select a person and spend some time observing their body language and what this tells you about them, and whether it enhances or detracts from their impact. As mentioned earlier, try watching TV with the sound off while analysing those on screen.

- Shoulders forward or back?
- Eyes sharp and focused or vague and distant?
- What kinds of hand gestures occur?
- Head straight or tilted?
- Hands restful, fidgeting, folded?
- Face expressionless or animated?
- Smiling, scowling or neutral?

Your body language

You may be terrific at reading other people's body language yet how aware are you of your own? Do you enter a room slouched, as if apologizing for your size? This applies equally even if you are relatively short in stature. Do you enter head held high and walking tall, even if you are not?

How congruent are your gestures with what you are saying? For example, do you tend to smile when talking about something serious or vice versa? Do you have a weak handshake yet a broad smile – these two contradict each other, sending out confusing messages.

Similarly, next time you are with someone and smile at them, check your hands and arms. Are they relaxed or tense, in a clenched fashion or folded across your chest? Again, these may be sending conflicting messages.

Inner attitude and commitment to your message heavily influence how your body behaves to support your communication. If you feel positive, believing strongly in what you say then it is likely that your hands will naturally do plenty of talking. If you are feeling negative or downhearted, your gestures will probably quickly give the game away, even if you stay absolutely still.

We are focusing here only on gestures – that is, bodily movements, rather than your general appearance, which is the subject of Chapter 8.

Several deliberate types of body movements may require courage yet can enhance your impact.

- **Communicating gestures:** These translate directly into words or phrases – for example, the OK sign, thumbs up, finger pointing, V for victory, waving the whole hand to mean hello and hugs. These can also have entirely different meanings depending on the local culture.

  Can you think of a communicating gesture that you use regularly? How could you incorporate a new one into your next interaction with someone, without making it seem artificial or forced?

- **Supporting gestures:** These illustrate your words – for example, circular hand movements, hands held when talking about something large, hands moving forwards decisively to suggest action.

  Are these something that come naturally or must you make a special effort to use them? In your next interchange with someone, experiment with some supporting gestures and discover both how these feel and what effect they produce in the audience.

- **Emotional gestures:** Movements of the face, hands and body suggest happiness, surprise, fear, anger, sadness, delight, thought – for example, stroking your chin while frowning.

  How easily do you convey your emotions through your physicality or do people find you hard to read? If you do not know the answer to that question it is worth exploring it further with people you trust. Deliberately allowing some emotion to show may feel challenging, but is part of removing the mask, making it easier for people to experience your impact.

- **Relationship gestures**: These influence another person, such as nodding your head to encourage them to continue talking, opening your mouth to show you want to say something, waving your open hand to tell the person to continue talking.

  This is another important piece of physicality to obtain feedback about. It can be hard to know if you are doing these movements as, often, they are done entirely unconsciously. For example, you may think you are neutral or even encouraging in your interactions with people, yet they may experience you as cold, rejecting or rude simply because you do not readily offer these essential relationship movements.

- **Personal need gestures:** These encompass scratching your nose, moving your hair from your eyes, doodling, shredding paper, removing some lint from someone's clothes, etc. They can prove effective in conveying concern for someone or in communicating your present mood. They are often complete giveaways as to how you are feeling and are not easily controlled. For instance, if you regularly doodle, you may think it helps you concentrate on someone speaking. The reality is they may experience you as conveying boredom or disinterest.

  Next time you get into conversation with someone, take some time to check what personal need gestures the other person is making. Then go deeper and try to catch the ones you make too.

  Since these gestures are so involuntary, rather than trying to rigidly control them, it is better to practise increasing your attention and focus on the other person, then usually these movements will take care of themselves.

> it can be hard to know if you are doing these movements

These different types of physicality provide a vast range of possibilities to enhance your impact. Not only can they convey your message wordlessly, they can give it added strength through emphasis or lack of it. However, you have to be willing to use them, since not all come automatically.

Face to face

Facial movements alone can communicate many basic emotions, including happiness, surprise, fear, anger, sadness, disgust, contempt, interest, confusion and determination. People with a strong Charisma Effect tend to be brave and allow their face to reveal their emotions, often relishing this display.

 Face work out

Stand or sit in front of a mirror. With only facial movements, express surprise. What signals it? You will probably notice things like raised or curved eyebrows, wide-open eyes, a dropped-open mouth and so on.

Now try and do the following.

1 **Intensify** your gesture of surprise – exaggerate it as much as you can.

2 **Underplay** your gesture of surprise – what is the least movement you can make and still convey surprise?

3 **Disguise** your surprise – cover up or hide your feeling while still experiencing it inside. Imagine someone has just told you some exciting or wonderful news but for various reasons you cannot let them know you are pleased.

4 **Mask** your surprise – substitute your expression of surprise with an entirely different emotion.

The importance of these is not that you learn to be an actor. It is your awareness that there are different ways of conveying your feelings facially and if you use them incorrectly you may appear insensitive.

By regularly practising people watching you can begin raising your awareness of gestures and body language. Try to decode the message from the person you are watching while ignoring their words.

People have been communicating through body language for over a million years but it has only been studied intensively in the last 30. Trying out gestures and attempting to alter your body language to be more positive or impactful can feel quite challenging, until it becomes more part of who you are.

The main point to absorb, though, is that using your physicality comes more naturally when you speak from the heart – that is, with conviction. In many ways your body language will take care of itself, once you become entirely focused not on yourself but your audience.

 ## Body language work out (in private)

1　Stand where there is enough space to move your body freely without feeling cramped or hemmed in.

2　Keeping your facial expression neutral, use your entire body to express each of the following states:

angry; ashamed; casual; dominating; impatient; modest; questioning; surprised; suspicious; undecided; disinterested.

3　Now allowing your face to adopt appropriate expressions, use your entire body to express each of the following states:

resigned; doubtful; shy; ashamed; modest; sad; aloof; self-satisfied.

4　What was the difference between these two performances – one with no facial expression and one with? How difficult was it to convey the state without using an obvious facial expression? Did your body gestures tend to follow your facial expression or the other way around?

5　What have you learned from doing this work out? What does it suggest to you about using body gestures to support your message and enhance your impact?

'If you didn't get frightened, you shouldn't be out there.
It keeps you on your toes and keeps you alive. It
doesn't stop you.'

Ellen MacArthur, fastest woman to single-handedly
sail round the world

Chapter 7
Passion

'The best leaders I know are passionate about what they do,' reported Alan Leighton, Chairman of the Royal Mail, after interviewing some of Britain's top business people. If the word 'passion' makes you queasy, then how do you feel about commitment or enthusiasm?

Research conducted by British Professor Richard Wiseman studied participants of FameLab, a national competition to find the new 'faces of science'. Those most able to transmit their emotions to others progressed furthest in the competition, using their personalities to impress a panel of judges.

Despite its known power to affect oneself and others, there is nothing spooky or beyond reach about passion. Often it is just a case of reconnecting with a long-forgotten part of oneself, which has been allowed to atrophy. At other times it is a case of allowing one's commitment to shine through.

> there is nothing spooky or beyond reach about passion

Passion is not only useful when talking about your major life interest, it is also valuable for communicating about less exalted, day-to-day issues. For example, when discussing with a client your company's service, you will be more effective if you show a genuine commitment to that service and want to share it.

You will make more impact when you feel an issue is really important and convey this through using your natural enthusiasm. Passion has the ability to influence other people's emotions, thinking and even behaviour. So it is worth exploring your own self-awareness around this whole issue.

Not sure about your passion, what excites you or gets the adrenalin flowing? Try the various work outs below to look more closely at your life and the key events that made you the person you are.

 ### Firm up your passion work out (1)

Looking at the past

1 Use the picture below to draw your lifeline. Create your own large version, if possible at least A3 size.

2 **For home and life in general**, including interests and hobbies, plot the highs and lows, events that caused you joy or sorrow, made you proud, excited, etc.

   Show the strong, transition points when things fundamentally changed you, making you the person you are today.

3 Which of these events made the most impression and why?

4 **For your career**, make a second chart and plot the highs and lows, the points where you felt most excited and where you were most bored or demotivated.

Timeline 1: How did I get here?

Firm up your passion work out (2)

Looking to the future

1   Use the same A3-size paper to *look ahead just one year*. List what you would most like to change in each of the areas you recorded on the previous chart.

2   *Now try looking ahead three years.* How would you reach these things and what steps would you need to take to reach these goals? Start dreaming about your aims. Don't worry if they seem fanciful or even impossible.

3   *Finally, look ahead a full five years from now.* What would your life look like then? What will have changed? What could you do to make it happen?

4   Use the timeline to write down your thoughts and feelings about the various issues you have recorded.

5   What are some of the underlying themes? What seems to be present no matter what the situation? What values seem to matter most in your timeline?

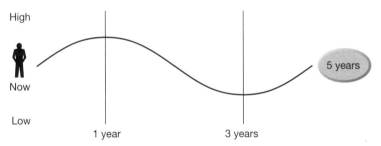

Timeline 2: Where do I want to be?

Firm up your passion work out (3)

Using the information you produced in work outs 1 and 2, complete these two sentences.

The core values that guide my life which I live by are

....

The one important thing you should know about me is

....

These two simple statements can provide a reference point when you are communicating with others and want to make a strong impact.

They are not necessarily words you will actually say – though you may sometimes want to do that – they provide a mental baseline for your communication and what matters to you.

These three work outs will help you think more intensively about your life, your passion and what fuels it.

People who use passion to communicate tend to do the following.

- Persist at getting their message across. Most people don't have a sudden revelation about how to do it, they just have to keep working away at it.

- Accept that they probably won't get their communication right immediately. Start with the nearest statement you can get that describes your passion and go from there.

- Realize you have found your passion when you reach the point where you are only satisfied if you can excite others with your enthusiasm. That is, you know what you want and will not settle for less.

When you succeed in showing your passion in communication, people will experience you as purposeful, enthusiastic, confident or conveying self-belief, spontaneous, ready to challenge, energized, excited, having a sense of fun and playfulness. These can be contagious, exerting a magnetic quality, drawing people to you and building your impact.

Aim and passion

As Chapter 1 explained, achieving a clear aim is an important first step on the journey to creating a strong personal impact, but clarity alone is not enough. Like a car engine being prepared for an important race, your purpose needs to be supercharged – not with petrol but with your passion.

> passion turns an intense spotlight on aim

Passion turns an intense spotlight on aim. Strength of purpose turns out to be one of the most enduring and distinguishing features of successful people with impact. They love what they do and explaining what really matters to them, which is why they come across so well.

Questions to ask yourself

- Is my purpose in communicating really clear?
- Do I feel strongly about this purpose?
- Would I enjoy explaining it to other people?
- Can I convey real passion for this purpose?

Enthusiasm and passion

Many people can be passionate about their aim yet do not fully convey how strongly they feel about it. This is where enthusiasm comes in. Allow yourself to show excitement about your purpose and share it with people. In this way you appeal to both their heads and their hearts.

Genuine enthusiasm is nearly always infectious, and the more uninhibited you become the greater its likely impact on others. Obviously, you can overdo the 'look how excited I am' form of communication and consequently make some people feel uneasy. Yet, on balance, it is better to be over-enthusiastic and risk a negative response than to play it safe and keep your passion under lock and key.

It is a myth that people, especially the so-called reserved British, frown upon enthusiasm and therefore it should be avoided at all costs. This usually only occurs when people become so over-excited it seems they have lost any sense of reality.

Questions to ask yourself

- Am I excited about what I wish to communicate?
- What exactly excites me about this issue?
- Why should other people be excited by it too?

Confidence and passion

Do you ever wonder about the secret of those people who seem to exude confidence and self-belief? How do they do it? Is it upbringing, high status, wealth, education, career success or what? As explained in Chapter 3, confidence does not simply happen. It is a result of practice and through acquiring competence that ultimately confidence is generated.

When you fully connect with your passion or commitment, though, it can automatically start to build your confidence. This happens because in sharing your passion you are, in effect, practising speaking about what really matters to you. That in itself can build confidence.

Once you become entirely absorbed by the meaning of your message, you cannot easily contain yourself, which leaves little space for feeling nervous.

> ### Questions to ask yourself
>
> ● How confident am I about what I want to communicate?
>
> ● Why does the issue I want to communicate matter to me?
>
> ● Why should it matter to others?
>
> ● If I was totally confident, how would it affect what I say?

Spontaneity and passion

When you act openly, with spontaneity, you are likely to create an atmosphere that is equal and honest. If people see you speaking from the heart, not just from the head, it can be infectious, often prompting them to act that way too.

How comfortable are you thinking on your feet and accepting things as they come? Do you feel nervous, preferring to stick closely to whatever actual or mental script you have chosen?

how comfortable are you thinking on your feet?

Lack of practice provides one common reason for being fearful of thinking on one's feet. Unless you graduated in advanced physics, if someone asked you to talk without preparation to 500 people for 15 minutes on Einstein's Theory of Relativity you may well find it difficult. Yet it is seldom lack of knowledge that makes thinking on one's feet such a challenge.

Or perhaps you believe that thinking on your feet requires a lightning response, a razor-sharp brain producing instant insights? This may be true if you want to be a stand-up comedian improvising on the spot or someone engaged in clever repartee. Generally, thinking on your feet merely requires you to stay in touch with what you care about and therefore enables you to draw on your inner resources without restraint.

While spontaneity cannot by definition be entirely planned, you can fertilize the ground in which it flourishes, through anticipation, listening, questioning, big picture thinking and buying time.

- **Anticipation**: There are many situations in which you can predict you may need to act spontaneously, without having a formal route map to follow. For example, you may be asked to give an instant speech, talking off the cuff about something. Humorist Mark Twain boasted it always took him several weeks to prepare a good spontaneous speech, meaning that he was always ready in some way for these challenges.

- **Listening**: People will often provide you with important clues and information about what they are thinking and feeling. Through attentive listening and watching, you can usually pick these up so you become ready to respond when necessary.

- **Big picture thinking**: Whatever issue is under discussion, try and see it with fresh eyes, extend your thinking. For example, when searching for a response try asking yourself: 'What is this really about?', 'What might be missing here?', 'What does this remind me of?', 'How does this relate to my own experience?', 'What is this issue telling me about the situation I now face?'

- **Buying time**: Give yourself more room to be spontaneous through buying time before you respond.
  - Wait for a speaker to completely finish before attempting to give a response.
  - Offer a question of your own.
  - Ask for some thinking time.
  - Make noises such as 'hmmm' to show you are paying attention but are still thinking.
  - Use filler phrases like 'That's a good point', 'This could have lots of implications', 'We need to talk more about this.'

- Reflect back on something the speaker has said, 'So what you seem to be saying is ...'
- Without offering an immediate response, tell a story that reminds you about this issue, while continuing to think how best to respond.

Questions to ask yourself

- Am I willing to be spontaneous in getting across my communication?
- What might get in the way of my willingness to act spontaneously?
- How can I best prepare to make the most of certain likely situations?

Challenge and passion

When you encounter people with a passion or commitment they tend to question ways of doing things, have strong opinions on certain situations, press for action and in many cases show an uncomfortable readiness to rock the boat.

Driven by their passion such people seem courageous, yet in practice they are simply committed to their aim. In pursuit of it they are willing to confront, raise uncomfortable issues or question what is happening. Yet underneath these same people may be anxious or unsure of themselves.

How you challenge is as important as the challenge itself. If in doing so you make the other person wrong, feel disrespected or in some way attacked, this may undermine, rather than enhance your impact. Try challenging as if in search of information:

- 'Is that how everybody feels right now?'
- 'What can we do to change this situation do you think?'
- 'This does not seem right to me, what are your views on this?'
- 'Where do we go from here?'

- 'This seems wrong to me – anyone else feel the same way?
- 'Would it be possible to do it differently next time?

The more you allow your passion free rein, the more you need to ensure your challenges spring from a positive source, rather than defensiveness, lack of confidence or a desire to make someone else look bad.

Questions to ask yourself

- Why do I need to challenge?
- When did I last make a challenge using my passion?
- What kind of challenges am I unwilling to make and why?
- Who am I least willing to challenge and disagree with?
- Do I challenge from a position of seeking information or do I tend to challenge so that people feel attacked?

Energy and passion

To communicate with passion and enthusiasm demands energy. It is energy you put into how you speak and behave. You cannot convey passion for your message while talking in a boring monotone, sitting slumped in your chair, not looking people in the eye or allowing your head to drop to your chest as if half asleep.

Energy used to convey passion takes many forms, including your physicality – how you move and act, your voice, smiling or, in some cases, your mastery of public speaking.

> energy used to convey passion takes many forms

When you exhibit a high level of energy it helps make you visible, establishing your presence. If you feel this is a relevant issue for you, then set out to become more aware of your energy levels at different times and notice that when these seem low, this tends to reduce your ability to convey commitment.

Without energy even the most powerful message or most persuasive speaker will go unheard.

Questions to ask yourself

- When was the last time I really used energy to convey commitment or passion for some message?
- Do I regularly put energy into how I convey my essential messages?
- How is this energy mainly displayed – in gestures, voice, visual appearance?

Fun, playfulness and passion

Using passion does not mean you must always come across as deadly serious. It may be equally effective to have fun talking about your passion by creating a sense of playfulness around it. For example, you might use your natural humour to get across your strong message or refuse to take yourself too seriously and create a sense of enjoyment around conveying your core message to people.

Ways to generate a sense of fun and playfulness around your message are limited only by your imagination and your readiness to take risks. This might include singing your message, reading a poem, wearing a funny hat, dressing up, audience participation, telling a story against yourself, using interesting words, metaphors or stories, cartoons, movie clips, in fact just about anything that allows you and your audience to see the amusing side of things and receive your message.

Passion is the future

We have seen that to enhance your Charisma Effect a vital ingredient is being able to identify and fully use your passion. Reassuringly, the world is gradually moving in that direction too, with more and more awareness of its importance not just for the individual who needs to make an impact, but entire organizations.

As Gary Hamel, the widely respected commentator on business puts it, the future of companies in the twenty-first century is to build an environment that 'cherishes human initiative, creativity and passion.' Using your passion is exactly what your colleagues may really need, and when you properly exploit it you will certainly make a powerful impression.

'One person with passion is better than forty people merely interested.'

E. M. Forster, novelist

Chapter 8

Demeanour

I f you are a pop star or an eccentric millionaire you probably do not need to worry much about your general appearance and manner – your demeanour. But if you are neither, then it can seriously affect your personal impact.

Demeanour is a handy, if rather posh, word for your manner. This includes how your carry yourself, your grooming, general appearance and image. Each has an influence on how people experience you and each may need some attention as part of making sure you make the best of being yourself.

> demeanour is a handy, if rather posh, word for your manner

For example, in an eight-year battle over patent infringement the judges complained that an expert witness potentially lost all credibility 'due to shifty eyes and poor demeanour'. In his swan song budget in 2007, the then chancellor Gordon Brown, conscious of his reputation for being dour and controlling, put on a jaunty demeanour by cracking jokes and affecting a light-hearted manner.

A successful warehouse manager for a major UK electronics company really looked the part. Complete with shiny suit, slicked down hair and pointy shoes, he felt fine with his appearance, until he got an important new job working for the BBC, where he was expected to present to senior executives. His unchanged appearance now proved too alien to the culture of the organization he had joined. His inappropriate demeanour undermined his ability to make an impact.

Being neat, clean and fresh may seem enough. Perhaps you are also someone who believes substance counts more than outward appearance? However, because people initially have little else to go on when making judgements about you, your general demeanour can be all-important.

How would you describe your outward appearance? Would people call you well-dressed, dapper, smart, stylish, conventional, or merely drab and ordinary? What is the image you want to convey, not just on those special occasions when you take particular trouble to look good? When you put out your clothes to wear, either on the day or in preparation for it, what is the impression you want to make? Who is the person you want people to encounter? Try the appearance work out below.

 Appearance work out

Find a full-length mirror, as in a department store's changing rooms. (Consider installing one at home as part of improving your demeanour.)

Wearing your normal work clothes, look long and hard at what you see in the mirror. This is different from the earlier mirror work out in Chapter 1. In this work out, view yourself for care, flair and aware.

● **Care**: Does the person in the mirror seem to take care of themselves? What are the signs of care – for example, crumpled or fresh looking, shoes scruffy or smart? Hair a mess or orderly? What changes would you recommend to this person about their appearance?

● **Flair**: What makes you look distinctive? Does anything stand out or is everything bland in terms of look, colour or design? What changes would introduce some flair – for example, more or fewer colours, higher-quality clothing, more stylish look?

● **Aware**: How appropriate is your appearance to your working life? Does it fully align with the message you want to send people about your charisma and the impact you want to make?

Does your image suit the job? Take, for instance, a go-ahead young woman executive from the music industry who attended one of our Personal Impact courses. She held a responsible job in her company, having graduated from art school, yet in sartorial terms she had never really moved on. She continued dressing in excessively tight-fitting blouses that, while fine back at college, now made her look a flirt.

Using video and a mirror, and perhaps with a little external feedback, you can make a useful start to improving and strengthening your demeanour. As with your overall communication purpose discussed in Chapter 1, start thinking about the following.

- What image do I want to project?
- What image do I fear projecting?
- How big is the gap?
- How can I eliminate the gap and still be me?

Take, for example, Peter D, who started as an independent management consultant. With an already persuasive Charisma Effect, he began achieving meetings with senior company executives, yet he wore cheap suits from high street chain stores. Meanwhile those he hoped to advise usually dressed in stylish, costly gear that enhanced their obvious status.

Eventually, an experienced fellow consultant kindly explained: 'If you are going to deal with senior people who wear immaculate, distinctive apparel, you cannot get away with looking cheap.' Peter immediately went out and ordered two top-of-the-range business suits. From then on he never looked back, confidently dealing with his growing list of prestigious clientele on equal terms.

Awareness work out

1   At your next team or business meeting take a systematic look at how people are dressed and their overall appearance. Does it enhance or undermine their impact?

2   Contact three trusted friends or colleagues to ask for frank feedback on your grooming.

3   Ask them to describe how they see your general dress sense. Would they describe it as stylish, dapper, careless, casual, low key etc.?

4   Next ask them to say how they see your general grooming, such as clean, neat, attention to detail etc.

5   Next ask, 'Do I have any annoying habits or gestures that you think might get in the way of making a strong impression?'

6   Finally ask them how they see your physical appearance, such as overweight, thin, stooped, upright, good bearing etc.

7   Obtain a video camera and film yourself entering a room and standing – what message do you seem to project, are your clothes appropriate, what works about your appearance?

8   Use all this information to make changes in your general grooming.

Demeanour may sound like jargon and be hard to nail down precisely, but starts with first impressions. Based on them, people make assumptions about your:

- economic status – rich, poor, successful, average
- educational level – graduate, basic attainment, drop out
- trustworthiness – honest, believable, reliable
- social status – quality, high-flyer, mixes well, oddball, loner, moving up or moving down
- level of sophistication – cool, confident, anxious, at ease
- attitude – aggressive, friendly, easy-going, hard to know.

Such judgements can occur in seconds, which is why demeanour can be so critical. One study of recruitment, for example, found good grooming actually produced more favourable hiring decisions than actual job qualifications.

Let's put this whole issue of demeanour on a more business-like footing. What are you willing to invest in your appearance and manner? It may be a cliché to talk of personal branding – as if you were a bar of soap or a car – yet this remains a useful benchmark for assessing your willingness to invest in yourself and how you come across.

> what are you willing to invest in your appearance and manner?

- How strong is your brand (your image)?
- What does it need in the way of a refresh or an upgrade?
- Does your brand speak quality?
- Can you afford not to invest in it?

When appearance does not fully match your desired brand image it is time to invest in change, but this does not mean altering your entire personality. To improve your personal impact means spending time and resources on developing various aspects of general demeanour. This could include your wardrobe, posture, grooming, handshake, manners, image and so on.

Your wardrobe

This is the most obvious area where you can make rapid changes. For example, if you are a man, do you stick to a drab palette of black, grey, blue and the occasional khaki-coloured neutral? If you are a woman, are you frightened of wearing clothes that could be construed as showy rather than functional?

High-powered women in particular will often firmly declare that, 'I am not interested in fashion', implying that senior women are supposed to be above it all, that fashion is for secretaries and lesser mortals. Dig deeper and they will often reveal a yearning for being able to dress fashionably.

While it may be unhealthy to let fashion rule your life, to ignore the power of clothes is nothing to be proud of either. In fact it could be a form of arrogance or a sign of being out of touch with reality.

There are seven common mistakes that people make about their clothing.

Mistake number 1: Cheap and cheerful

If you are determined to improve your impact quality, it is an investment, not extravagance, to buy quality, especially in the business world. Cheap is ultimately expensive; not only because it can harm your image, but in the simple cost per times worn.

Mistake number 2: Ignore fashion

Certain fashion looks date you, and you ignore these at your peril. It is no use saying, 'I am not interested in fashion', since it is not you who cares, it's your audience.

Fashion is confusing, transitory but rather less arbitrary than you might think. Today, all fashion alters so quickly that, paradoxically, one of the best solutions is to invest in a classic look that refuses to date. While more expensive in the short term, classic looks pay back handsomely in the longer term.

Mistake number 3: Poorly fitting clothes

If they fit badly, even the best clothes can be a disaster. A good fit is so essential it is worth paying the extra tailoring cost to get what you want.

If you want to look well turned out and noticeable, common mistakes like items being too tight, the wrong length or a strained fit, are unacceptable.

Mistake number 4: Lack of co-ordination

Make sure your clothes blend in with each other correctly or the whole effect can be entirely ruined. Colour co-ordination can make or break a person's appearance, so give this area of your grooming some thought.

If you do not entirely trust your instincts to buy items that go together appropriately, consider investing in learning about the basic principles of colour co-ordination. There are some simple guidelines, such as how to ensure the colour in a major item of clothing also reflects minor accessories; when to put a light item with a dark item; when one colour does not go with another; or what colour best suits your particular complexion. These can all help improve your co-ordination.

Mistake number 5: The other bits don't matter

Accessories are the small details that make a statement. Badly chosen ties, hat, bag, belt, gloves, shoes, socks and even an umbrella can potentially damage your image and you may never know it.

Make sure accessories underpin not undermine your image. For example, items of jewellery can be dangerous territory for a man, especially someone wanting to climb the corporate ladder. A glittering earring may be acceptable on a famous footballer but will it help your impact too? For women, flashy belts, garish jewellery and face studs can be fine outside of work, yet seriously reduce your personal impact in the work arena.

Mistake number 6: Small image killers

Like inappropriate accessories, small image killers leave a nasty taste and yet can easily be prevented, once you become aware of them. Here are some to avoid:

- fraying – collars, cuffs or signs of wear
- badly pressed clothes – do not impress

- spots – on ties, dresses or suits
- buttons missing, loose or undone
- jacket sleeves or trouser lengths too long or short
- shoes – scruffy, unpolished or in need of repair
- shabby belts.

Mistake number 7: Do not be distinctive

In the early history of computer giant IBM, just about every man – and it was only men in those days – wore the company uniform of blue suit, white shirt and carefully matching tie. The days of IBM clones have mainly gone but, with the exception of start-ups and high-tech firms, there remains a huge pressure on employees within many organizations to conform and avoid standing out from the crowd. Yet it is a mistake to assume your wardrobe must be entirely bland and impersonal.

> it is a mistake to assume your wardrobe must be entirely bland and impersonal

Making yourself invisible is no way to enhance your personal impact. Being distinctive and stylish should be perfectly possible, even within the limitations set by the conventions surrounding you. Look for creative ways to make your clothes really reflect who you are and not solely how others apparently want you to be. Apart from clothes, your demeanour also consists of how you carry yourself, including grooming, your general expression – do you smile a lot or mainly frown – how you walk, your general bearing and your social manners.

Getting help

Not everyone has a natural flair for clothes and style. The only thing worse than not having it is not having it and not knowing you do not have it! As with all areas of self-awareness the great secret is really not a secret at all – get honest feedback.

To obtain feedback on your clothes and style there are plenty of specialists around from colour experts to personal shoppers in large department stores, from fashion and style advisers to one-to-one coaches who focus on the whole area of personal impact, including working on appearance. You will find some useful sources at the Charisma Effect website (www. charisma-effect.com).

The social sins

A famous charismatic stage and film star once invited a young unknown actress to dinner. Not only did her guest fail to appear, but neglected to apologize or explain her absence. Some days later, the two women unexpectedly met at the Museum of Modern Art in New York. 'I think I was invited to your house to dinner last Thursday night', the young woman began. 'Oh, yes?' replied the star, 'Did you come?'

Manners may no longer quite top the bill for success these days, but they remain an important factor in affecting your demeanour. Don't reserve your best behaviour for special occasions. You can't have two sets of manners, one for those you admire and want to impress and another for those whom you consider unimportant. For a strong demeanour they need to be same for everyone.

Since manners are simply artificial rules, they can be broken under the right circumstances. For example, in England people usually expect men to remove their hats indoors. However, if wearing a stylish hat is your personal fashion statement then you may be able to get away with this, using it to build your particular personal impact.

Here are seven common deadly social sins.

1   Failing to say thank you when someone has shown you an act of kindness.

2   Sitting badly in meetings, including rocking back and forth in your chair.

3 Being overly familiar with someone without permission.

4 Not treating people with respect.

5 Touching objects or people without direct encouragement.

6 Continuously interrupting or loudly dominating the airwaves.

7 Disparaging someone in front of someone who matters to them.

The point about manners is they need to be appropriate, showing respect for your audience.

Personal grooming

Now let's get really personal, I mean the territory that only your best friends or someone you fully trust dares enter.

Brian was sent on the road by his company to learn about the basics of selling and distribution. His job was to visit small retail chemists and take restocking orders. In one shop, after talking at length to the owner, the latter politely invited him to come to the back room, where spare stock was piled to the ceiling.

In the privacy of this unpretentious space the owner said quietly: 'Brian, has anyone ever told you that you have extremely bad breath?' Brian's eyes widened in horror; no one had ever said anything like that, ever. 'Well you do, young man, and I urge you to do something about it. It could do you lots of harm on your way up the ladder.' To his credit, Brian responded with gratitude to this feedback and immediately visited his dentist to sort out the problem, which turned out to be a gum infection.

When Gordon Brown was chancellor, press photographs of his severely bitten nails went round the world. True, it did not stop him becoming prime minister, but it weakened the image of an otherwise apparently confident man in charge of the nation's finances.

To check your image, do the personal grooming killers work out opposite.

Personal grooming killers work out

Take an honest look at yourself and only tick the boxes if you are sure.

		✓
BREATH	Is your breath fresh?	
	Would anyone actually tell you if it was not?	
HAIR	Is your hair washed, ungreasy and in a modern style?	
	No wisps trying to cover up bald pates?	
TEETH	In reasonable order; fresh looking?	
FACIAL HAIR	Carefully attended to, including ears and nostrils?	
	No unruly, unflattering, untrimmed, unshaven areas?	
CHEW GUM	You don't!	
CLEANLINESS	Are your nails, face, hands, all visible areas well scrubbed?	
NAILS	Are these well-cared for, not bitten or chewed?	
DANDRUFF	None in evidence (there is no excuse these days)?	
SKIN	Fresh and healthy looking, not sallow, flaky or greying?	

We are so used to our own bodies that it can be hard to recognize when something begins to affect our personal impact adversely. This really is best friend territory and it is worth asking someone you trust to tell you frankly whether you are experiencing any of the personal grooming killers.

> this really is best friend territory

My colleague, Michael Maynard, who has helped countless people develop their potential and their Charisma Effect, argues that the key point about personal grooming is, 'It's about care. Do you look as if you take care, and do you look cared for?'

Posture

Avril, an experienced headteacher and assistant director of education, kept applying for jobs as a director of education in large English local councils. She was constantly shortlisted for interviews, yet kept failing to win the high-level job she wanted.

Personal coaching revealed her habit of entering the interview room with her head down and slouching – it was as if she was apologizing for even being there. Her mental attitude, partly influenced by her negative posture, ran along the lines of, 'I wonder if they will appoint me this time.' The combination of the two directly affected her demeanour and reduced her Charisma Effect.

In one-to-one coaching, Avril learned to walk tall, with head held high. She began entering the room while imagining she was *already* a director of education and was attending merely to answer a few questions, using her expertise and experience. Transformed, Avril used the learning at her next assistant director interview and was duly appointed.

As a child, Queen Victoria was trained to keep her chin up by the presence of a prickly sprig of holly under her collar. The postures of Elvis, Nijinsky, David Bowie, John Wayne and Prince all contributed to their particular Charisma Effect. Even though we tend to pay less attention to the importance of posture these days, it can still directly affect demeanour.

You can gain from some outside feedback, either in a one-to-one coaching session or in a workshop dealing with postural and other issues. For example, watching yourself come through a door to meet a group of strangers can prove a revelation.

If you spend hours hunched over a computer, it is a fair guess your posture will suffer. We see many people with heads poked forward and walking badly due to excessive screen time. Most people think standing straight consists of tensing the back, heaving the chest in and up and pulling one's head towards their chest. This is not so. The spine has two natural curves that you need to maintain: from the base of your head to your shoulders and the curve from the upper back to the base of the spine. Consider learning the Alexander Technique with a qualified teacher. This proven method prevents stoop and unnecessary muscle tension. It helps regain natural posture and adds a quality of ease to the way you move and work.

If you feel pain, especially back pain, when trying to attain a good posture or suffer from back, neck or pelvic injuries, do not attempt to correct these yourself. This could cause further damage. Contact your doctor or visit an Alexander Technique teacher before trying to tamper with your alignment.

Posture work out

- When standing straight up, make sure that your weight is evenly distributed on your feet, both forwards and sideways. It might feel as if you are leaning too far forward, and look stupid, but you don't.

- Push your shoulders forward, then bring them straight up, then straight back, then down. Feel good? If your shoulders feel slightly stiff or tense you may have unnecessary muscle tension.

- If your head hangs forward you cannot be properly aligned. Keep your head at a level that allows you to look directly ahead without having to turn your eyes up. If this causes tension in your neck you are in need of some retraining.

  - Align ears with shoulders.

  - Raise both arms out to sides at shoulder height.

  - Hold for a slow count of 10.

  - Slowly lower arms to sides, counting to 10 as you lower.

  - Do 10 repetitions, constantly checking your alignment! If 10 reps are too many to start, do as many as you can. You should at least feel a slight fatigue in the shoulder muscles.

▶

- Be a penguin. While waiting for a web page to load, toast to pop up or the microwave to beep, place elbows at your side and touch your shoulders with your hands. Keeping your hands on your shoulders and your ears aligned, raise both elbows sideways, count one, two and lower them back to your waist, count one, two. Do as many reps as your wait allows. You'll be surprised how much exercise fits into 30 seconds.

'To live is not just to survive but to thrive, with some passion, some compassion, some humour and a little bit of style!'

Maya Angelou, writer

Part 3

Chemistry

Create that special attraction

This third part of the A-B-C approach to improving your Charisma Effect introduces three essential components, summed up as A-I-R:

- **A**ttention
- **I**nterdependence
- **R**apport.

Each contributes to creating chemistry, which is all about building a relationship between you and your audience.

Chapter 9

Chemistry:
the need
for A-I-R

The recruitment consultant puzzled over her client's hesitation to accept the two scientifically trained candidates just interviewed. Each matched the search criteria, so why was the client hesitating? 'I just don't feel comfortable appointing either of them,' she explained apologetically, 'they both have the personality of a concrete slab.'

The search agent was even more confused. 'But personality was never mentioned in the search criteria, we just thought they had to be fully qualified and fit in with your culture.'

The client nodded, 'I know, but they must at least be persuasive in this job, otherwise they will be stuck in the lab for the next 10 years. I can't see either of those two getting on well enough with people.' The agent reluctantly agreed and the search process began again, this time clearly specifying an ability to build relationships with people.

The crucial comment made by the client reminds us that it is not just about your aim, or your behaviours, but about how you get on with others. A positive, lasting impression depends on the relationship you establish with other people. 'It is more important to click with people than to click the shutter', remarked *Life* magazine photographer Alfred Eisenstaedt.

Chemistry and charisma publicly surface in the entertainment world where reviewers repeatedly point to an explosive mix:

chemistry and
charisma publicly
surface in the
entertainment world

Tom Cruise and Katie Holmes, Brad Pitt and Angelina Jolie, Jackie Chan and Chris Tucker are just some of the recent chemistry charisma stories.

Similar stories occur in the business world but often in the reverse direction with frequent reports of the chemistry breaking down. One of the most spectacular occurred when Hewlett-Packard's charismatic CEO Carly Fiorina clashed with her board and was summarily fired in 2005.

Chemistry explains why certain people's Charisma Effect produces such an impact while others struggle to make an impression. Unfortunately, you cannot easily watch chemistry happening because it involves invisible signs such as the arousal of the sympathetic nervous system, rising blood pressure, a feeling of weakness in the knees and psychological arousal combined with a feeling of pleasure.

Yet we certainly notice when chemistry goes missing. People say, for example, 'there was no chemistry between us', meaning nothing special happened. Remember the last time you felt an instant affinity with someone – a sense of shared perspective, a connection or unexpected harmony that turned a new acquaintance into a colleague or a friend? Or, remember when you simply 'clicked' with someone. That was chemistry in action.

Equally, you can probably recall first encounters you would rather forget, where the failure to 'click' created unsatisfying experiences such as poor teamwork, bad project co-ordination, blighted career prospects, pointless meetings and less than rewarding interactions at work.

While it would be great if we could all easily click with each other, luckily meetings and human interactions can still occur without the need for any obvious chemistry, so long as people feel reasonably comfortable with each other. They convey their messages to each other and move on. The absence of anything special between them hardly matters. At the supermarket, for instance, you may hardly exchange more than a few sentences with an unknown checkout person; beyond superficial politeness, neither of you expects much personal chemistry.

Similarly, at work, you might drop into a person's office who you know only casually. Having passed on some item of information you leave after only a brief conversation and without any real chemistry occurring – there is no meaningful relationship.

At work, chemistry matters because it makes interactions between members of a team more satisfying and productive, meetings can be in-depth with openness and real warmth. Better still, individual members will be more likely to share vital information or come to each other's aid.

In our private lives, most of us gravitate towards those with whom we get on well, where personal chemistry seems to happen. And the reverse is usually true.

 Chemistry in action work out

1 Think of a specific time when you got on really well with someone. It could be when you made a new friend, thoroughly enjoyed working with a colleague, talked with pleasure to someone for the first time on the phone, spent time with a favourite client, etc.

2 Think back to that occasion and try to relive it.

3 Recall how you felt at the time, what sorts of things happened and what kinds of things you said to each other.

4 List the things that suggest there was chemistry between you. For example:

we both smiled often; we had fun; it felt really creative; there was plenty of laughter; we seemed to agree about nearly everything; we couldn't stop talking; we joked whenever we disagreed; there was such a lot of mutual respect, the atmosphere felt electric ...

....

....

....

....

....

....

5 Which of these could you actually see (i.e. behaviour) and which were to do with intangibles like feelings or mood?

6 Now find an occasion devoid of chemistry. What was missing? What were the feelings or mood?

Because we mainly experience personal chemistry, rather than directly observe it, we cannot readily set a target for it, make it into a company metric or nail it down with numbers. Organizations requiring their people to achieve certain competencies cannot realistically insist everyone achieves a 70% level of chemistry with each other!

In fact we only fully realize the existence of chemistry between people through the strength of their relationships. Understand how to build productive relationships and you will possess one of the vital keys for enhancing your Charisma Effect.

there are some highly practical ways to encourage the creation of personal chemistry

Because chemistry seems such a touchy-feely topic it is easy to dismiss it as firmly in the territory of how to win friends and influence people. Indeed one famous attempt to make sense of it suggested it all came down to having a healthy body. But things have moved on since then and we now know there are some highly practical ways to encourage the creation of personal chemistry.

You need A-I-R

To start or maintain a fire you need three essential elements: heat, fuel and air. Remove any one of these and the whole thing collapses – the fire goes out. Much the same applies to chemistry in the Charisma Effect. It involves three essential key elements working in combination:

RAPPORT

Use this easy to remember A-I-R mnemonic to guide you in your experiments with personal chemistry.

In the next three chapters we explore the implications of this approach.

'Seven years would be insufficient to make some people acquainted with each other, and seven days are more than enough for others.'

Jane Austen, author, from *Sense and Sensibility*

Chapter 10

Chemistry: Attention

Meeting Bill Clinton, a UK colleague remarked that the ex-president, 'always makes me feel as if he has flown across the Atlantic for the sole purpose of talking to me.'

Giving someone your absolute attention is one of the most flattering and devastating tools at your disposal. It is an important catalyst for stimulating personal chemistry with the power to transform people's feelings and behaviour.

When you give someone your absolute attention, because your entire focus is entirely on them, you have no time to be insecure or awkward. Remember the challenge of entering a room full of strangers mentioned earlier? By concentrating on what other people are doing, how they are standing and talking, analysing what is going on, deciding who best to talk to first, you leave little space for deadly negative thoughts, anxiety or self-consciousness.

> when you give someone your absolute attention, you have no time to be insecure or awkward

Giving someone your absolute attention is akin to putting on a set of horse blinkers to stop yourself being distracted by your surroundings. The person you are talking to fills your vision entirely and you cannot easily be diverted. No peering over the other person's shoulder to see what else might be happening, no half an ear listening to a nearby conversation. Your entire focus remains laser-like on the person with whom you are engaging.

Complete attention consists of far more than looking fixedly at someone's face. When giving someone absolute attention you maintain regular eye contact, look genuinely interested, use and remember the person's name, listen attentively, smile, encourage the person to talk about what interests them, and make the person feel important, valued and respected. These have to be real, not fake. As you practise them they will cease to feel forced and gradually become part of how you normally act towards other people.

Eye contact

Casanova – writer, philosopher, raconteur, entrepreneur, diplomat, adventurer and lover – was a great communicator. He had a formidable Charisma Effect. When, belatedly, he met his own daughter he complained bitterly: 'How could you have recognized me, if you did not look at me? If only you knew, my angel, what unforgivable rudeness it is not to look at the person to whom you are talking. Who could have taught you such a bad lesson?'

Psychologists today talk of young children being socialized through mixing with their peers. They assume most will learn naturally how to use the Charisma Effect and, for example, look directly at someone when you talk to them, but reality is different. Many young people never fully learn these skills. Sadly, computers, iPods, television and social websites prove no substitute for experiencing live face-to-face communication with another human being.

We have 'lost the art of properly socialising the young' commented Peter Wilby, a writer at the *Guardian*.[1] In fact, the socializing process proves faulty for many people who reach adulthood; they grow up puzzled and perhaps hurt at not always making the impact they expect.

---

[1] Peter Wilby writing in the *Guardian*, 'Britain has lost the art of socialising the young', 1 August 2007.

'People are attracted to people who are attracted to them,' explains Ben Jones from the Face Research Laboratory at the University of Aberdeen. 'It's a basic effect that we are all, at some level at least, aware of – which is when you smile at people and you maintain eye contact, it makes you more attractive.'

Dr Jones and his colleagues say attractiveness relies on social cues that convey 'I am interested in you.' The most important cue seems to be whether someone is looking directly at you.

When you really pay attention, normal eye contact consists not of staring fixedly at someone, but regularly catching their eye and holding it there for no more than just a few brief seconds. However, two factors also make a big difference as to whether or not this enhances the Charisma Effect.

The first factor is Dr Jones' findings that a direct gaze is only attractive if the person giving it looks as if they like you. The second is the need to be aware that in some cultures direct and prolonged eye gaze may be disrespectful or unacceptable. You need to take both these factors into account when using eye contact. The first means you need to actively 'transmit' your preference for someone if you intend using eye contact to make a real impact. Second, it means that using it without regard to people's cultural expectations can actual damage your impact.

Eye contact exerts an invisible grip – you can hardly underestimate its power. If you did the mirror work out in the Introduction you will recall how those eyes staring back at you could be disconcerting, even though they were your own!

eye contact exerts an invisible grip

Eye contact work out

Think of someone you have met who appeared unwilling to look you in the eye and seemed instead intent on looking everywhere else.

Using single words or just a short phrase, how did this make you feel?

....

....

....

....

- Did you get on well with this person at the time?
- How long did you remain in their company?
- Were you glad or sorry to part from them?

When you use eye contact well, it is both the direction of your gaze and its length that matter. So, for example, you could also look at someone's mouth, their nose, chin and eyes and still suggest eye contact. Equally you can look away thoughtfully for a moment and return to make contact and it will still indicate continuous contact and therefore interest.

Eye contact is such an important contributor to personal chemistry because it sends those silent messages such as 'I really like you', 'I find you fascinating', 'Well, what do you think?', 'It is your turn to speak', or even, depending on your accompanying expression, 'I am not happy about what you've just said.' No wonder they call the eyes the windows to the soul.

Eye contact comes naturally when you genuinely show attention. What matters is both your intent and intensity, but an unwavering stare can almost be as bad as no eye contact at all.

If you genuinely show attention, without hiding behind note taking, tapping at a laptop, fiddling with a mobile or being distracted in some other way, your attentive eyes will take care of themselves, being alive with direction, focus and openness.

You probably already know about the value of regular eye contact, but do you really practise it or do you tend to reserve it for special occasions, generally looking away, dodging normal contacts? Next time you talk to someone, try holding their gaze a little longer than normal, without of course looking as if you are trying to wear your eyes out.

Look interested

Chemistry has a lot to do with very primitive parts of our brain and the laws of sexual attraction in particular function at a subconscious level. However, as we have already seen, chemistry is certainly not confined to sexuality.

To look interested you need to *be* interested! While that can seem challenging at times, it is why so many successful people with a strong charisma effect make such an impact. They manage to be really interested in you, even if only briefly.

The signs of being interested are well known – you can nod, lean forward silently, make encouraging sounds such as uhuh, mmm, ahh and so on. But doing these in a forced way will only reveal you are faking it. Instead, try letting these gestures well up naturally from the depth of your interest.

On certain occasions taking notes can also show your interest but not if it removes your attention away from the other person for more than a few moments.

Use and remember names

'Er, Mr Pridmore, would you say you are a forgetful person?' was the question asked of newly crowned world memory champion in 2004. British-born Ben Pridmore, who can recall the order of a randomly shuffled 52-card deck in 26.28 seconds, happily replied: 'Oh yes, I forget everything. I go into a room and wonder why I am there? Happens to me all the time.'

As brain expert and writer Tony Buzan, who organizes the world memory championships explains, 'The first reason why people forget, is that they haven't paid attention in the first place.' That particularly applies to people's names. The sweetest sound in the entire world is said to be hearing one's name being used in conversation. Apart from showing you are paying attention, using someone's name also sends the message that you think they are important. Not using their name really does send the opposite message.

> not using their name really does send the opposite message

People commonly complain of a terrible memory for names, while still being aware that names matter. Yet remembering names has far less to do with memory loss than with ignoring simple techniques to make names memorable.

Unless you have an actual medical condition, you can improve your recall for names with some easy, tried and tested ways.

- **Desire**: You must genuinely want to remember the person's name.
- **Stop and listen**: Too often, we meet someone and immediately launch into another conversation.
- **Use the person's name**: Do this two or three times during the conversation. Each time you use a person's name during conversation you will be more likely to remember it. Try saying:

- 'Good to meet you Daniel, this is my first time here, what about you?'

- 'With experience like that Daniel, I imagine you get to travel quite a bit?'

- 'It was a real pleasure talking to you Daniel; maybe we'll get a chance to chat again some time.'

Don't overdo the repetition; more than three times in a five-minute conversation would sound forced.

- **Verify**: unless the person has introduced him- or herself to you, check what he or she wishes to be called.

At a conference or seminar, for example, the name tag gives you an excuse to use the person's name. However, it may have been typed incorrectly or they may prefer a more formal or informal version of the name they like to go by – ask them.

If someone else introduced you who does not know the person well, ask what they prefer. For example, 'Jeff introduced you as Debbie, is that what you prefer to be called?' This will both cement the name in your mind and ensure you use one that pleases them.

If the person's name is unusual, or could be spelled in more ways than one, ask the person how they spell it.

- **Picture**: According to brain experts, most of us try remembering names the wrong way. We think of them as lists or sounds, when we should be thinking in terms of images.

One president of the United States continually amazed his many staff by remembering all their names. His method was to imagine the person's name boldly printed on their forehead.

Try visualizing the person's name in as many interesting ways as you can – for example, their name scrawled on their forehead in your favourite colour using a marker pen or flickering in red flames filling a clear blue sky. Alternatively, associate their name with a picture, the more bizarre the better – for example:

- Samantha – a sexy, black panther
- Jack – climbing a bright red beanstalk
- Thomas – the front of a Tank Engine
- Joshua – blowing down the walls of Jericho
- Grace – a gazelle, gracefully lolloping along
- Ruby – stuck inside a giant ruby and trying to get out.

The more strange and extreme the picture you use, the more likely you will recall the name later.

- **Write:** Write down the person's name. If that seems inappropriate at the time, just imagine yourself noting it down; create a feeling of actually writing with tiny hidden hand movements, while saying the name silently in your head.

  Later, actually write down the person's name three times, while picturing the person's face.

- **Face files:** When meeting someone for the first time, find something striking about their facial appearance; perhaps their nose, large forehead or lips. Ignore hair or glasses because these can change over time.

  Say their name to yourself, along with their facial characteristic. For example, John with the long nose, Peter with the narrow lips, Mike with the dimple on his chin, Melanie with green eyes.

Listen attentively

One day in 2001, film director Roman Polanski called Robert Evans the producer and recent author. He complained he had been in a car accident and his new Mercedes had been destroyed. 'What happened?' Evans asked. 'I was driving down the Champs-Elysées listening to your new book,' Polanski explained, 'and I was laughing so hard I crashed into a tree!'

As Polanski found to his cost, if you are listening really attentively it is best not to be doing something else simultaneously. At work, while someone is talking to you, you cannot expect to make a strong impact if you continue tapping at a keyboard, check for messages on your

> if you are listening really attentively it is best not to be doing something else simultaneously

mobile, scribble distractedly in a notebook and fiddle with a desk toy.

Have you an inner voice that annoyingly pops up when you are trying to give someone your full attention? I mean the kind of inner voice that mutters irrelevant or negative thoughts or provides a running commentary on what is happening? If your reaction to this is 'I don't have an inner voice', that's it! The one that just said you don't have an inner voice.

How do you turn off the inner voice, so you offer undivided attention? Here is one way to switch it off. When we engage in inner talk, we tend to move our tongues, even if only imperceptibly. So, try putting the tip of your tongue to the roof of your mouth, interrupting the negative inner talk pattern. Sounds simple? Try it!

You can also quell distracting thoughts through becoming fully absorbed by the other person, fascinated with their expressions, use of language, way of talking, humour, opinions and the rest.

Listening takes up more of our waking hours than any other communication activity. Yet most of us receive little help with how to do it properly. Here is the single most important tool you can use for listening attentively:

● have a definite purpose in mind.

When you choose a clear reason for listening intently it transforms ordinary conversation into a more meaningful dialogue. You stay fully alert for clues, signs and information that may guide you in your response.

For example, you may decide to listen for specific information, to solve a problem, to understand, to encourage. You may also have secondary purposes such as listening for key phrases, descriptive or emotive words, tone of voice, pace of speech, speech patterns, metaphors and use of images. All of these may reveal what the person is thinking or feeling and suggest how you might respond appropriately.

People have two ears and one mouth, which is a good reminder to spend twice as much time listening as talking. Active listening consists of both internal and external action. Internal action is what you do to stay alert and present – for example, having a specific purpose in mind while you listen. External action is when you send back clear verbal and non-verbal messages to the other person, so they realize they have your undivided attention.

During attentive listening to encourage personal chemistry, your responses need to be mainly positive, rather than negative. For example, avoid ones that suggest:

- ordering – 'Do this', 'not that'
- deterrence – 'Don't do that because …'
- preaching – 'You must …'
- advising – 'I suggest that you …'.

Be an active listener

- **Face the speaker:** Through body language show your attentiveness, sitting up straight or leaning forward slightly.
- **Maintain comfortable eye contact:** Avoid letting let your gaze wander to other people or other activities taking place.
- **Minimize external and internal distractions:** Turn off your laptop and mobile; ask the speaker and other listeners to do the same.

- **When they speak, respond by showing you are listening:** Murmur 'uh-huh' and 'um-hmm' and nod. Raise your eyebrows. Acknowledge the speaker's point by making comments such as, 'really' or 'interesting'. Also include more direct prompts, such as 'What did you do then?'
- **Focus solely on what the speaker says:** Try not to think about what you want to say next.
- **Watch for non-verbal clues:** Notice what the speaker does as much as what they say.
- **Keep an open mind:** Avoid making assumptions about what the person is thinking or what they will say next.
- **Avoid offering gratuitous advice:** Just assume the person needs to talk it out, until you get asked a specific question suggesting help is needed.
- **Listen for key words or phrases:** These are the ones that suggest feelings or emotion.
- **Engage:** Ask questions for clarification without seeming to conduct an inquisition.
- **Reflect back:** Try playing the mental game of never offering your own view until you have first summarized aloud your understanding of what the other person has just said. Use reflecting phrases like 'you said', 'you mentioned', 'you suggested before', 'you described'.
- **Don't interrupt:** This can be tough, but with practice you will get better at it. Even when there is a pause, don't jump in with your contribution. Wait to see if the speaker has really finished.

Active listening work out

1   You meet someone in the office who says: 'I've just been talking with our glorious leader and, guess what, he wants us to speed up the rate we deal with enquiries from the other departments.'

▶

2 A close colleague at work admits she cannot talk to another member of the team: 'No matter how hard I try, he never seems to listen or take me seriously. I've tried getting angry, but he just laughs it off and changes the subject.'

3 At a meeting with a new client you hear: 'I personally would rather not go out to tender, but it's part of our procurement policy and this project will attract a lot of scrutiny, so I suppose it's unavoidable.'

In each of the above scenarios:

● rephrase this person's comments more succinctly

● express your understanding of what the person means

● what questions could you ask to clarify any potential misunderstandings?

Smile

There is an old Indian saying: 'The smile you give out comes back to you.' People respond to smiles, they are contagious and hard to resist. People with a strong Charisma Effect often smile a lot because they have found how effective it can be in demonstrating their attention.

If you are a natural, frequent smiler just go on doing it. You already know it builds charisma. But some of us find smiling does not come easily and we have to work at it. Rather than smiling at random, watch and listen for something to trigger your smile, like the other person smiling, a clever point made in their conversation, an emotive adjective ('we had a *wonderful* time'), a colourful phrase ('sales have gone ballistic') and so on.

false smiles, however, can be almost worse than none at all

False smiles, however, can be almost worse than none at all. When you fake a smile certain facial muscles do not move, while others around the eyes only move when you feel genuine emotion. You have little control over these physical giveaways, but as observers we are trained from birth to instinctively notice them.

There is solid research showing that smiling releases certain chemicals in the brain, leading to changes in relaxation and feelings of well-being. The more you do it the better you feel and, consequently, people will rapidly pick up on your mood and reflect it back.

Encourage talk about interests

In showing your absolute attention, make it apparent you want to learn what particularly interests the other person or group of people. You need no excuse to ask about this, it is what happens when people try to get to know each other better and build a relationship – they exchange increasingly personal information.

- 'Are you working on anything really interesting at the moment?'
- 'Faced any exciting new work challenges recently?'

Since asking about interests can be potentially intrusive, do it with care. One way to start the ball rolling is by sharing some of your own current work or social interests and see if they resonate with the other person.

Act as if the person is important

People like to feel valued and respected; you convey this by giving them your absolute attention. For example, you take what they say seriously, giving it obvious thought. Rather than immediately disagreeing with their point of view about something, make it clear they are entitled to their opinion even if you don't share it. Ask them about their views, the problems they see or the reservations they have.

In a work setting, many senior people expect to readily gain attention because of their role rather than who they are as human beings. While not ignoring their role, show your attention by being interested in them as a whole person rather than their status or position of power.

'We had a lot in common. I loved him and he loved him.'

Shelley Winters, actress in *Bittersweet*

Chapter 11

Chemistry:
Interdependence

T wo of the most powerful personalities in the dance world came together in the duo of Margot Fontaine and Rudolf Nureyev. Each was already a star and used to hogging the limelight, yet they set out to make the other look brilliant and talented. Each entirely depended on the other for their success and in doing so strengthened their impact beyond anything they could have achieved individually.

The Fontaine–Nureyev on stage romance represented a generosity of heart. Both gave themselves up fully to the other, until they were working in such harmony that even their separate gestures and movements aligned

> even their separate gestures and movements aligned without conscious effort

without conscious effort. They had become entirely interdependent.

Interdependence is the second of the three A-I-R elements that generate chemistry as part of the Charisma Effect. It is:

- a constantly changing two-way experience, relying on both parties to make it work.

If you have ever successfully collaborated with someone or a group of people on some activity you will have experienced interdependence. It is the absolute opposite of what happens in many companies, where people often work in silos, cut off from each other.

For example, in one major hotel chain we worked with, all the various departments operated separately; different groups had built their own empires. No one seemed to realize, for instance, that room service depended on catering and housekeeping to be successful. It was hardly any wonder the service was poor and there was virtually no interdependence between those supposed to deliver it.

If you know you depend on others for your mutual success then you will almost certainly approach the situation differently than if you assume you can do it alone. For example, if you act as if you are dependent on the other person you will tend to think about what is in it for them, as well as what is in it for you.

Recent research, shown in the table below, suggests what makes a person good to collaborate with.

An ideal prospective collaborator

	Overall rank
Indispensable characteristics	
Is enthusiastic about the subject of collaboration.	1
Is open-minded and curious.	2
Speaks their mind even if it's an unpopular viewpoint.	3
Very important characteristics	
Gets back to you and others in a timely way.	4
Is willing to enter into difficult conversations.	5
Is a perceptive listener.	6
Is skillful at giving/receiving even negative feedback.	7
Is willing to put forward unpopular ideas.	8
Is self-managing and requires 'low maintenance'.	9
Is known for following through on commitments.	10

Source: Copyright © 2005 Mitch Ditkoff, Dave Pollard, Tim Moore and Carolyn Allen, *The Ideal Collaborative Team* (available at http://blogs.salon.com/0002007/stories), reprinted with permission.

Collaboration requires both parties to take action that directly affects the other: for instance, showing enthusiasm, being open-minded and curious and being willing to speak your mind.

Like navigating a fast-flowing river, interdependence means you must watch out for the equivalent of hidden currents, sandbanks, reefs and tides, that could take the relationship dynamic off course. To do this, keep exploring questions such as:

- How can I be sure I am satisfying this person?
- At this moment what does this person need?
- What is *not* being said that could be important?
- What strong feelings do I detect in others and in myself?

How can I be sure I am satisfying this person?

Chemistry means creating something where you and those you interact with leave feeling satisfied in some way. It is the same experience you enjoy in good company during a pleasant conversation in the pub or in some other informal setting. You both leave feeling enriched in some way.

When you actively look for what will satisfy the other person you are not simply pandering to their excessive demands. It is more a case of trying to uncover what the other person wants from the relationship.

At this moment what does this person need?

This takes 'satisfying the other person' action a stage further. Now you use your ability to be fully present and alert to detect what the person wants right now: for example, to stop arguing, have a breath of fresh air, turn on the television, talk frankly, trust you, hear your advice.

ask the other person if you have assessed their need correctly

Often the best way of uncovering the answer will be to test out your own assumptions by asking the other person if you have assessed their need correctly.

What is *not* being said that could be important?

This is potentially one of the most powerful actions you can take to promote interdependence and move the relationship from the initially superficial to an entirely new level. For example, you may detect that, although the conversation is progressing perfectly amicably, there is actually an undertone of dissatisfaction, impatience or mistrust that is not being expressed.

People often say one thing and mean another, and to build interdependence and promote chemistry you may need to get beyond guesswork to move the relationship onto more solid ground, based on good communication and mutual trust.

What strong feelings do I detect in others and in myself?

Emotions, both yours and other peoples', play an important part in the Charisma Effect and influence the extent to which you generate a sense of interdependence.

Some people are brilliant at detecting how others are feeling while remaining out of touch with how they themselves feel at the time. Similarly, others may be good at knowing what is going on inside themselves during an interaction, while being unable to detect what others may be experiencing.

A good guide is:

- if you detect how someone is feeling, check next how *you* are feeling and if there is a match

- if you detect how you are feeling, check how you think the *other* person may be feeling and if there is a match.

Connection

You can also promote interdependence through a connecting type of conversation in which you try to reach a shared agenda.

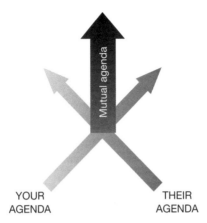

YOUR
AGENDA

THEIR
AGENDA

Seeking a connecting conversation

Connecting conversations may start off far apart. However, by consciously seeking links and opportunities to collaborate, you and the others move closer together, gradually building interdependence. Somewhere along the way, you locate a crossover point where you find a mutual agenda that encourages the natural chemistry between you. At its best, the results are greater than the sum of their parts.

Here are five easy to apply principles for encouraging interdependence.

● Principle 1:   Accept and build
● Principle 2:   Make the other person look good
● Principle 3   Reciprocity
● Principle 4:   Avoid making the other person wrong
● Principle 5:   Name it.

Principle 1: Accept and build

The most obvious example of accept and build in action is when people have brainstorming sessions. When these are well run, criticism or negativity about other people's ideas are relegated to later. In the early stages, everyone makes suggestions and people are encouraged to build on each other's contribution.

accept and build is taking what someone says and working with it constructively

The essence of accept and build is taking what someone says and working with it constructively. That is, you keep adding value to their suggestions or what they have said. You do not necessarily have to agree with them: for example, you may choose to take the idea in a different direction.

Remember the game *Consequences* that you may have played when you were younger, where someone drew a picture, folded it and passed it to someone else who added something new to it? Or when one person wrote the first line of a story and the next person added constructively to it in some way? Accept and build works like that – during a conversation you listen for opportunities to elaborate constructively on the person's own idea.

A particularly good way to trigger accept and build is to keep using the phrase 'Yes and ...'.

Accept and build in action

1 'Why don't we shut the office and spend an afternoon together on the river?'

- 'Yes and we could also each bring an item of food to create a team meal.'
- 'Yes and someone could bring an MP3 player with a speaker for some music.'
- 'Yes and we could ask people in advance for what music they want.'

2 'I think it's time we had a new brochure.'

- ● It could also be time to redo our website.'

- ● 'While we're doing that why don't we ...'.

3 'The office is starting to look a mess again, time we had another collective tidying session.'

- ● 'We could try hiring someone to do it for us!'

- ● 'I could organize a waste collection for that day too.'

- ● 'Personally I like the mess but I will gladly bring in some music to cheer you up while you're doing it!'

Principle 2: Make the other person look good

By deliberately trying to make the other person look good you become part of their success, generating interdependence. Here are some examples of doing that.

- ● In a team meeting someone asks a question. Rather than simply giving the answer, instead you take the opportunity to make them look good by saying: 'That's a really good question. You always get to the root of things' or 'I bet that's given us quite a lot of food for thought.'

- ● When introducing a client to a colleague, you find something that makes them look good: 'This is Mary who runs the customer care department. She has an absolute passion for keeping customers happy.'

- ● In a team argument about some proposed action, you find a way to show that both parties who seem far apart are really saying the same thing and both have a good point of view.

When interdependence goes missing not only does the chemistry fail to work but it can also create the equivalent of a chemical explosion. Try completing the nightmare scenario work out.

Nightmare scenario work out

1   You are jointly presenting at a conference with a colleague who drops their notes and entirely forgets what they were talking about.

● *How could it go downhill from here – for you?*

....
....
....

● *How could it go downhill from here – for the other person?*

....
....
....

● *What would interdependence look like where you support each other and together win?*

....
....
....

2   At an important meeting with senior colleagues you suggest an idea for a project that conflicts with one just proposed by someone else.

● *How could it go downhill from here – for you?*

....
....
....

● *How could it go downhill from here – for the other person?*

....
....
....

● *What would interdependence look like where you support each other and together win?*

....
....
....

Making the other person look good is rather like having a public love affair that stays firmly in the work setting and never carries over into private life.

Making the other person look good

1 A colleague or subordinate has not achieved an agreed goal.

- Rather than: 'You failed to achieve this goal, which is totally unacceptable in this company.'

  Say: 'You didn't hit the target but must have learned a lot along the way. What have you learned so it won't happen again?'

2 A client gets the wrong end of the stick about your product.

- Rather than: 'No, you've misunderstood, it can't do that.'

- 'That's a really interesting point, which hadn't occurred to me. Let me explain briefly again how it works and why it probably wouldn't do what you are suggesting.'

3 A colleague is really angry at not being promoted.

- Rather than: 'I never thought you would get it. You just don't have enough experience yet.'

- 'Well at least you put yourself out there, now they know for sure you're serious about making a difference here.'

In an interdependent relationship you put your focus on the other person. You are committed to their success and vice versa.

Principle 3: Reciprocity

When people get on with each other there is genuine give and take. Without it not much of substance happens between human beings. Since you may not always know if a person wants to build a relationship with you, simply assume they do and use the basic principles of reciprocity shown in the diagram.

> **IT'S RECIPROCAL**
>
> • To gain attention
>   *be attentive*
>
> • To become interesting
>   *be interested*
>
> • To be understood
>   *seek to understand*

These are easy to remember when interacting with people. For example, if you wonder why others fail to find you interesting or seldom want to spend much time talking to you, could it be because you do not show enough interest in them first?

As we saw earlier, giving someone your absolute attention builds your personal impact. Most people like talking about themselves and if you seem genuinely interested it can be irresistible.

Principle 4: Avoid making the other person wrong

you offer a new perspective, an alternative view or a different interpretation

This works like making the person look good. Rather than contradicting them, finding fault or suggesting they have got something wrong, instead you offer a new perspective, an alternative view or a different interpretation.

For example, suppose someone in a presentation shows a slide with a percentage column that seems to add up wrongly. Rather than pointing out their mistake and making them feel small, you find a different way: for example, 'Does this column add up to more than 100% due to rounding errors perhaps?'

Principle 5: Name it

You share your view of what might be happening in the relationship and invite the other person to work with you on interpreting the situation. For example:

- 'Does anyone else beside me feel a need for a break?'
- 'Seems we're going over the same ground, shall we move on?'
- 'You sound frustrated with my response; shall we talk about it?'
- 'I sense quite a bit of confusion about this.'

Encouraging interdependence does not always come easily, particularly to highly creative people who want to feel in control of their work and who find collaborating an uphill struggle. Yet even the most creative artists have gained from interchanges with others in bringing their work to fruition.

In organizations, leaders often appear reluctant to allow interdependence to surface and without realizing it undermine their own Charisma Effect. For example, when business guru Gerald Robinson tried to sort out a National Health Trust for a TV reality show, one of his first actions was to insist the elusive and low-profile trust's chief executive came with him as he walked the floors of the hospital to actually meet and converse with frontline staff. This seemed a revelation to the chief executive.

Interdependence is a creative process

For many people the whole idea of interdependence can seem strange, even alien. After all, most of us are constantly trying to establish ourselves as independent beings, able to stand on our own. Interdependence can appear to pull in the opposite direction.

It is through the creation of interdependence though that we build something bigger than ourselves, joining with others to produce something greater than the sum of the individuals. In doing so we become closer to others as human beings, promoting the essential chemistry of the Charisma Effect.

'When we start to live as brothers and sisters and to recognize our interdependence, we become fully human.'

Archbishop Desmond Tutu, Nobel Prize winner

Chapter 12

Chemistry:
Rapport

Oprah Winfrey, the American talk show host and entrepreneur, thrives on building a close relationship with her audience through telling stories and self-revelation. Among her early tales was that she had taken drugs, been raped as a child and, while struggling with her ballooning weight, had once eaten a jumbo pack of hotdog buns, drenched in maple syrup.

Adam Levine, lead singer and guitarist for the pop group Maroon 5 also has a tremendous rapport with his fans, 'But it took him eight years to develop,' said his mum. 'At his first performances, he performed with his back to the audience!'

Rapport is the third part of our A-I-R mnemonic for stimulating personal chemistry. It is an emotional bond or friendly relationship between you and other people. Based on mutual liking and trust, it creates a sense that you understand and share each other's concerns. Both parties feel an intense connection. Perhaps the greatest benefit comes from its ability to create a sense of satisfaction and completeness.

> it is an emotional bond or friendly relationship between you and other people

Familiarity differs from rapport, though some people confuse the two. Strangers sometimes accost celebrities in the street believing they actually know them well, but, instead of a real relationship with another human being, they are only familiar with a TV image.

You cannot engineer rapport, which usually occurs spontaneously when people 'click' with one another. However, you can certainly build the right conditions for it to flourish – for example, by being trustworthy, giving back to people more than you receive and showing respect. It is like strengthening a bridge over a river. The stronger the bridge, the more it can carry.

Each of us builds relationships with people in our own way; relationship building is an art, not a science. Essentially you use your whole person to communicate. What does that mean in practice? Useful principles for encouraging the creation of rapport between yourself and others include:

- connection
- sensitivity
- empathy
- respect
- physicality
- language
- asking questions
- offering help or information
- telling stories.

We will briefly explore each of these below.

Connection

To forge an instant connection with those you encounter, start using your natural curiosity to identify areas where you both have something in common. These might include feelings, ideas, experiences, views, contacts and values. Systematically uncover connections using your natural curiosity and intuition.

With the next three people you meet and converse with, try to discover three things you both have in common. Ignore the obvious, such as gender, the same employer or the present location. Instead, dig for unusual connections such as tastes, beliefs, experiences, hobbies, people you have met in the past, previous successes and failures.

It can be challenging to break into a group of strangers at some event to make new connections. It comes down to using good observation and some of the simple techniques shown in the box below.

Connecting with a group already engaged in conversation

- First, be willing to stand on your own without feeling anxious. You should not feel rushed into joining any one group.
- Select the group you want to join and note the intensity of the conversation.
- If people are 'locked' with good eye contact and positive body language step away from their immediate vision.
- Wait at a distance and watch for the conversation to change and join the group when it does.
- To start with, join in the conversation with your body and eye language; show interest only. Treat it like joining a film halfway through. With careful listening you will soon catch up. Maybe ask a few questions to show interest.
- Do not change the tone, pace or steal the conversation away from another person.
- Offer to shake hands only if the conversation turns to you and people are keen to find out who you are. If you have something important to say then do so at this point.

Be sure to respond positively to attempts by others to connect with you.

Sensitivity

insensitivity can act like strong weedkiller on a delicate plant

If you have ever said or done the wrong thing and realized your blunder, you will know how insensitivity can act like strong weedkiller on a delicate plant, ruining rapport.

You show sensitivity when you accurately assess other people's states of mind from a mixture of verbal and non-verbal cues. Increasing interpersonal sensitivity happens through steadily raising your awareness about:

- how you come across and the effect you have on people
- what people are thinking and feeling at the time.

It would be convenient if sensitivity was simply a technique, yet it is much more a process, a way of behaving where you are attuned to what people may be thinking and feeling: for example, being aware of cultural, gender, age, and racial differences.

To sharpen up your sensitivity, try the following.

- Avoid relying heavily on first impressions. Our natural tendency to judge someone is part of our survival instinct, but it can often let us down if we are too quick to draw conclusions about someone. Treat first impressions as assumptions needing further investigation.
- Make yourself open to new information and points of view, even when these contradict your most firmly held beliefs.
- Try to see things from the other person's point of view. Mentally stand in their shoes and see how your perspective alters.
- Watch out for and acknowledge differences such as culture, sex, race, age and disability.

Knowing how to retrieve the situation when your sensitivity fails is also important.

Empathy

Empathy helps create chemistry through shared feelings. You first get to grips with how others are feeling – you walk in their shoes and understand their situation and what they are experiencing.

For example, when you hear somebody talking about a frustrating situation, you connect with your *own* feelings of frustration. You can usually do this because often the person's story triggers a memory or a similar instance from your own life. In recalling the past situation you experience the original feelings you had at the time. This stirs emotions in your body allowing you to connect with the other person's feelings. All perhaps without you saying a single word!

Much the same occurs when people talk about their excitement when working on a certain project. Because most of us have experienced excitement and enthusiasm we already know these feelings. Empathy means you allow your feelings to be triggered by what the other person is expressing.

Here are some practical ways to communicate your empathy.

- **Avoid being judgemental:** Make it clear you are not evaluating or criticizing the other person, just trying to understand.

- **Listen attentively, with concern:** Maintain eye contact, hold an attentive posture and provide physical closeness; show your involvement with suitable facial expressions and gestures.

- **Reflect back:** Indicate to the other person the feelings you think they are experiencing so as to check on the accuracy of your perceptions. Offer tentative statements like 'You sound really puzzled about the team's motivations right now' or 'I seem to hear some doubts in your voice about our ability to deliver on time.'

- **Use self-disclosure:** Share your understanding through offering some personal information, but avoiding putting the focus back on yourself.

- **Make room for others to speak:** Do not fill the silence with your own thoughts or feelings. Empathy is often just giving the other person room to reflect and share.

- **Check back:** Watch for clues such as the person giving a nod or a phrase such as 'that's right' or 'exactly' to check that your response is accurate.

Empathy works best from a spirit of curiosity, a sort of deliberate ignorance. Rather than trying to assume what another person thinks or feels, or even means, you show you are simply listening using body language or by verbal clues such as 'hmm', 'go on', 'tell me more'. Empathy and being in a hurry do not mix. There are no short cuts.

> empathy and being in a hurry do not mix

Respect

A new chief executive of Boots toured branches to meet staff on the front line. From one member he heard about a faulty tap in the canteen that had not been repaired for years, and from another that the company's prices for health and beauty products were too high. On returning to his office he showed that he took these comments seriously by tackling the pricing issue – and, incidentally, making sure the tap was fixed too.

As the chairman of a large UK distribution organization put it, 'Respect is something you give, not something you get.' Building a relationship with your audience involves showing respect for other people and their points of view. Even when you strongly disagree or feel what they are saying is stupid or trivial, respect means you avoid making them feel bad or in some way demeaned.

Respect builds chemistry between you and other people. Body language alone can convey respect or lack of it. Showing respect includes not abusing the relationship by turning up late or being badly prepared.

There are opportunities to show respect and build relationships through recognizing important cultural differences.

- Recognize and face your own and others' fears of acting inappropriately with members of different cultures.
- Recognize differences between yourself and culturally different groups.
- Realize that within any given cultural groups there are many differences.
- Become more aware of the differences in the meaning of words that rarely convey exactly the same message across cultures.

Physicality

Even when you think you are sending suitably positive messages, your body may be calling you a liar. You never entirely control what your body reveals, which is why the more you can be your authentic self the better.

Matching or mirroring someone's gestures can have a profound effect on how they relate to you and works best when it happens naturally, as part of being closely interested in what they say. The moment you notice yourself doing it, or trying to do it deliberately, it feels like a trick. In that moment you lose all the other elements of listening, empathy and natural relationship building.

Experiment with using your physicality to help build the relationship, but do so with great care. For example, rather than trying to directly copy someone's gestures, instead try matching their energy and their breathing.

Mirroring back someone's body gestures is much valued by practitioners of neuro linguistic programming (NLP) and if you are interested in this subtle area of rapport building you may like to look more closely at what it offers.

Part of physicality is the power of sex appeal. For some people this is a major component of their Charisma Effect and they learn to use it for all its worth. The danger of setting out to use sex appeal to boost your personal impact is that it becomes an artificial and manipulative device for creating chemistry, rather than a natural part of one's physicality. People soon realize when you start being deliberately 'sexy' to enhance your impact and in normal working situations this can quickly generate resentment and damage the healthy development of chemistry.

Language

While it is true words alone may play a relatively minor role in communication (see Chapter 4) carefully chosen ones can certainly affect people's emotions and therefore also promote rapport.

flattery is like using a counterfeit coin

Paying a compliment, for example, can be effective, so long as it comes from the heart and is based on definite information. By contrast, flattery is like using a counterfeit coin: you may get away with spending it, but it could cause you serious damage if detected.

Advertisers know certain words such as new, easy, free, health, money and sex can affect people's feelings and thoughts. We each have our own set of words or phrases that appeal to us and trigger our emotions. You can set out to discover what words appeal to someone and use this knowledge to help build your rapport bridge (see Hot words of influence, opposite).

You can also undermine rapport building by certain forms of language or mannerisms, such as constant hesitations, over-emphasis, one-word answers, poor me and blamer language (see Chapter 1), overly polite statements, slang and swear words. Because some high-profile celebrities, such as TV chef Gordon Ramsey, lace their language with swear words does not mean you doing so will enhance your Charisma Effect. It is far more likely to dilute it.

Hot words of influence

Look for people's word hot buttons to incite physical and emotional reactions.

- **Proactive people** respond to words like: go for it, just do it, why wait now, take the initiative, what are you waiting for, let's hurry.

- **Reflective people** say things like: let's think about it, this will tell you why, we need to really understand, could, the time is ripe.

- **Goal-motivated people** respond to words like: achieve, enable you to, benefits, advantages, here's what you need to do, obtain, attain.

- **Problem solvers or avoiders** respond to words like: solve, avoid, fix, prevent, get rid of, it's not perfect, let's find out what's wrong, there'll be no problems.

- **Internally motivated people** respond to words like: it's up to you, I suggest you think about, try it out and decide what you think, only you can decide, you might consider, call.

- **Externally motivated people** use words like: others will notice, it has been approved by, well respected.

- **Change-averse people** respond to words like: in common, as you always do, unchanged, as you already know, maintaining, identical, exactly as before.

- **Change-minded people** respond to words like: new, totally different, unlike anything else, unique, one of a kind, completely changed, unrecognizable, shift, switch, brand new, unheard of, the only one.

- **People-minded people** respond to words like: people's names, I, feelings, thoughts, experiencing, this will feel good, for you, for others, the people, our team, our group; and personal pronouns like it, this, that, these, those, they.

- **Thing-minded people** respond to words like: things, systems, objects, process, get the job done, focus on the task at hand, the goal, the results; and impersonal pronouns like it, this, that, these, those, they.

Source: Adapted with permission from *Words that Change Minds: Mastering the Language of Influence*, 2nd edition (1997) by Shelle Rose Charvet, Kendall/Hunt Publishing (www.WordsThatChangeMinds.com).

Asking questions

To promote rapport, pose intelligent questions that give the other person an opportunity to shine. For example, use open-ended ones that encourage them to talk and share interesting information.

Open-ended questions discourage one word answers, such as yes or no. Instead, they leave plenty of space for the other person to elaborate.

- 'Tell me about your boss.'
- 'What is it you like about this place?'
- 'What do you think went wrong?'
- 'That's really interesting, can you explain a bit more.'
- 'How do you feel about that?'

The more attentively you listen, the more the right questions will enter your mind. With good preparation you may also be able to anticipate what questions your listeners might ask.

Intelligent questions promote rapport through confirming you have been listening, showing the quality of your thinking, and sharing your interest and concern. Really good questions also contribute to rapport building by being disguised statements of feelings or opinions.

- 'Has your strategy been a success?'

  At one level this just seeks information; at another level it says 'I think your strategy has been a success.'

- 'Shall we take a break from this meeting?'

  At one level this is merely an invitation; at another level it suggests 'I think we should take a break.'

- 'Are there strong business reasons for wanting to do that?'

At one level it is only an enquiry; at another level it says 'Before embarking on this course of action I think you need some strong business reasons.'

Beware of the permanent advisory syndrome (PAS) where you rush to go beyond posing useful questions to start gratuitously telling someone your opinion and what to do. Some people cannot refrain from gratuitously offering advice along the lines of:

- 'If I were you I would do this ...'
- 'What you need to do is ...'
- 'I'll tell you the solution, it's ...'
- 'The first thing to do is ...'

Management consultants often suffer from PAS, reducing their personal impact by insisting on always coming up with answers, whether or not the client really wants them.

Offering help on information

By volunteering information or your services you signal you want to build the relationship and hence promote rapport. It could be as simple as saying you will send the person an article or report they would find useful. Or it could be a more substantial commitment such as your willingness to help solve a problem the person faces.

Once accepted, offers create a sense of obligation or new closeness that can affect the building of the rapport bridge. The offer itself may be far less important than the fact it is being made from the heart, without attempting to manipulate the other person.

Telling stories

Al Gore's Charisma Effect was hardly visible when he ran for US president and lost. Instead he came across as wooden and without much real impact. Contrast this with his Nobel Prize winning campaign alerting the world to climate change. Through his engaging story-telling he radically sharpened up his Charisma Effect.

often their tales will reveal their vulnerability and humanity

Inspiring leaders know the power of telling true and often personal stories to affect people's emotions. Often their tales will reveal their vulnerability and humanity, opening the way to rapport with others.

Personal stories work because listeners feel more than just entertained, they see you in a fresh light, perhaps having had similar important experiences of their own. For some situations such as an interview, a conference speech, a sales pitch or a negotiation it could be sensible to prepare a story in advance to use at the right moment. Keep your stories short and to the point.

One of the secrets of good story-telling is not so much the content, or even its relevance, it is that you clearly enjoy the chance to share it and your listeners feel closer to you as a result. By story I don't mean making bad situations look good. It is about accounts that are engaging so that listeners feel they have a stake in your success.

Creating stories also helps us believe in ourselves. With a compelling story we reassure ourselves that our vision, values or plans to move on in some way, make absolute sense.

Secrets of telling a good story

From *Star Wars* back to *Casablanca* and Greek tragedy, great stories rely on several basic principles:

1 Someone listeners care about – your audience must be able to relate to the person's aims, struggles, vision or experience.

2 A reason for taking action – what needs putting to rights.

3 Obstacles – trials and tribulations to be overcome.

4 A turning point – a point of no return, things change.

5 Resolution – the person succeeds well or fails tragically.

This structure of a story dates back to Aristotle more 2,300 years ago and seems to reflect how the human mind likes to organize reality, with a beginning, a middle and an end.

'I think there's a natural chemistry between us as friends; and there's really no separation between the rapport that we feel when we're in conversation and when we're playing music, it's one and the same.'

Benny Green, jazz pianist

Part 4

Putting it all together

This final part brings together the different aspects of the A-B-C approach to offer practical ways of applying new thinking and behaving in order to strengthen your Charisma Effect.

The four-step procedure offers a systematic approach in which you prepare, select, experiment and review to focus on change and alter your impact gradually.

To help with applying the approach in real-life situations, there are four common scenarios to show how the A-B-C to strengthening your impact can work.

Chapter 13

Using A-B-C
in real life

The A-B-C of the Charisma Effect is a gentle, easy-to-use approach. Everything fits together and so long as you recall the basic three elements you will start to make steady progress with an increased awareness of what produces a powerful and lasting impression.

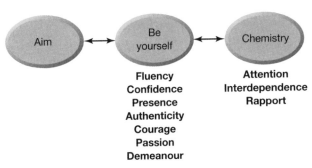

You cannot work on all of it at once, which is why exploring your profile (see Chapter 1) can be so useful in focusing on where to start.

There are two basic strategies you might consider adopting:

1 Focus on your known strengths and improve on them further.
2 Tackle specific development needs or weaknesses and work on these.

It is entirely your decision which approach you use, but usually some combination of both works best.

You can dip in and out of the various aspects of the A-B-C approach, using them as appropriate, but it could also be effective to use a four-step approach in applying it.

- **Step 1**: PREPARE to communicate with other people, including consciously holding the A-B-C framework firmly in your mind. Regularly remind yourself: Aim, Be yourself, Chemistry.

- **Step 2**: SELECT one of the key A-B-C behaviours or areas of development you want to work on – for example, confidence, passion, creating rapport, chemistry. Choose some practical actions to try out in the real-life situation.

- **Step 3**: EXPERIMENT with one or more of these new ways of interacting – for example using more open questions, more attentive listening, avoiding victim-type language or whatever.

- **Step 4**: REVIEW the results of your experiments. Consider further actions you might take.

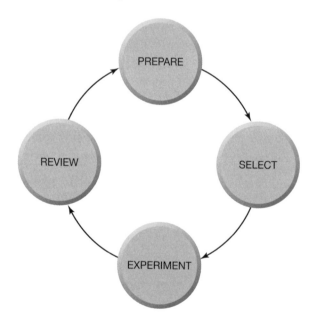

The A-B-C approach takes time to build into your regular interactions with other people, so avoid rushing it. Tackle the various issues you need to work at in very small bites, but keep at it, rather

> tackle the various issues you need to work at in very small bites

than leaving lots of gaps between your various experiments. In your daily interactions, keep checking on what is going on and what effect you seem to be having, how your audience seems to be thinking, feeling or behaving – reviewing the relationship dynamic.

At first, you may find it all a bit overwhelming as there is a lot to think about. As with all attempts at self-development it is usually best to avoid the 'big bang' approach of the New Year's resolution, setting an unrealistic target that is soon abandoned. Instead, go for small steps, constantly experiment and regularly review progress.

Eventually, the A-B-C approach becomes second nature – after all you are basically only reminding yourself Aim – Be yourself – Chemistry, then focusing on one or perhaps two aspects of this at a time. This is what many of those with a strong impact do anyway, without thinking; it is so ingrained it happens automatically.

Have a plan

It can also help to create your own development plan, working systematically through the A-B-C framework. Here is an example.

- On Monday, pay special attention to your Aim in communication; explore what happens in various situations and how clear you are being and whether others seem to be clear about your messages and intentions.

- On Tuesday, pay special attention to one chosen aspect of the Be yourself set of behaviours. For example, you may decide to work on presence, and within that you might explore using the presence highway code from Chapter 4.

- On Wednesday, select a second aspect of your chosen Be yourself behaviour to work on. So, if yesterday you chose the highway code, perhaps today explore the use of your intuition; check on whether it serves you well or not.

- On Thursday and Friday, work on one or more elements of Chemistry: Attention, Interdependence or Rapport.

- At the weekend, tune in to all three elements of the A-B-C framework and review how it worked during the week. What have you learned from applying the framework and how did it affect your personal impact?

Alternatively you could adopt a rolling programme in which in the first week you focus on Aim, the second week on Be yourself, the third week on Chemistry and so on. Whatever plan you select, follow it over several weeks to experiment and see what you can achieve.

Below are some typical challenges where people want to make an impact, showing the approach in action.

The A-B-C of social gatherings

While in many social situations you simply take things as they come, when you do not want to leave things to chance, the Prepare – Select – Experiment – Review approach can help maximize your Charisma Effect on these occasions.

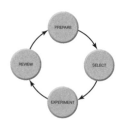

Prepare: Think of the A-B-C of the Charisma Effect and how you might apply this to the forthcoming event. Decide on a clear **Aim** for your attendance at this social situation. What exactly do you want to achieve, how would you know if you had achieved it? Can you produce a single headline summing up your intention? For example, your headline aim might be: 'To treat this whole event as if it were a surprise party for me.'

Two secondary aims, might be, for instance:

- 'To greet at least five people with energy and enthusiasm.'
- 'To look for opportunities to actively promote chemistry between me and one other person.'

What might get in the way of being yourself on this occasion?

Aim $\longrightarrow$ Obstacles $\longrightarrow$ Solutions

For instance, could your anxiety about making a good impression or your tendency to talk too much and not listen enough be obstacles? How might you overcome them this time? What solutions could you try on this occasion?

For example:

- 'I will focus all my attention on the other person's words, listening intently for what is not being said.'
- 'I will accept and build on anything the other person says' (see Chapter 11).

Select: The Be myself behaviour you might choose for this occasion might be courage, in which you set out to do what you would not normally do in making contact with other people.

You decide to take the risk of not being able to say anything much yourself in favour of listening intently.

Experiment: You might deliberately experiment with rapport-building methods such as non-verbal ways to encourage the other person to talk by offering nods, smiles and 'uh huh' sounds, which perhaps you seldom use much.

Review: Afterwards find some time to sit and analyse what really happened. How successful were you at achieving your main aim? If you were successful, what exactly made the difference this time? If it did not work out as you expected, can you identify exactly why not – for example, did your courage fail you in the heat of battle? What lessons are there for next time?

The A-B-C of presentations

Prepare – Select – Experiment – Review works well for helping to maximize your Charisma Effect on these occasions.

Prepare: Depending on your particular presenting strengths, focus your attention on your main presentation **Aim**.

As already shown in Chapter 1, AIM consists of two elements. First clarify the overall presenting purpose – your core message. What do you want people to remember from your presentation?

Use the basic starting point for clarifying your presentation aim:

Aim ⟶ Obstacles ⟶ Solutions

Devise a single headline describing your aim as a way to sharpen up your approach.

Second, use the CAN DO framework from Chapter 1 to further refine your thinking: **C**lear, **A**chievable, **N**eeded, **D**ivisible, **O**utcome.

What might get in the way of your presentation aim succeeding and how could planning overcome these obstacles?

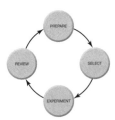

Select: Two of the A-B-C elements play a particularly important role in formal presentations – Aim and presence (see Chapter 4) – and have a disproportionately strong effect on how you come across. However, you may also need to work on some of the other A-B-C behaviours too. For example, authenticity may be an issue, requiring extra attention, or perhaps you will also need to develop your commitment or passion, or maybe confidence demands some attention. Refer to the relevant chapters in this book for these areas of concern.

Experiment: Use your new presentation to experiment with some fresh approaches and take some risks. This is the only way you can expect to develop and learn how best to enhance your impact in these demanding situations. For example, if your main area of attention is on presence, try using the presence highway code and see what effect it has on the audience and on yourself.

Review: After your presentation spend time reviewing what worked well and what did not. Did you complete your chosen experiments and what difference did they make to improving your personal impact? What else have you learned from this particular performance?

The A-B-C of meetings

Do you tend to call meetings and use your Charisma Effect or are you mainly a passive spectator?

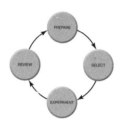

Prepare: There are various ways to strengthen your Charisma Effect in meetings. Start with the essential A-B-C reminder of Aim – Be yourself – Chemistry to organize pre-meeting thinking.

What is your meeting aim – for example, to have people really listen to your suggestions? Are there any secondary aims?

Aim ⟶ Obstacles ⟶ Solutions

What could get in the way of being yourself? Which of the Be yourself behaviours from Chapters 2 to 8 seem most relevant to your forthcoming meeting?

Limit your focus initially to just one of the seven behaviours, rather than on several, as this will tend to dilute your efforts.

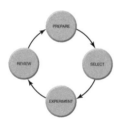

Select: There are two behaviours in meetings that often produce a large impact and these are confidence and fluency. Choose one that seems closest to your current need.

Use your charisma profile (see Chapter 1) to help identify which part of the A-B-C framework to focus on for this meeting.

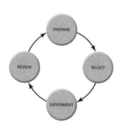

Experiment: Take a risk and try out an approach from this book that you have never tried before. For confidence, try using a new a mindset (see Chapter 3) that encourages you to approach the actual event positively. If you select fluency (see Chapter 2) use one of the various ways of developing this aspect of yourself – for example, by concentrating on the big idea and not allowing yourself to get lost in too much detail.

Review: What effect did these experiments have on those at the meeting? How did people react? Consider what further actions you might take.

The A-B-C of small talk

Does making small talk fill you with dread? Do you feel tongue-tied and awkward at the prospect of passing the time apparently chatting about trivia? You are certainly not alone in this. The A-B-C approach to strengthening your Charisma Effect provides a good foundation for approaching these situations.

Prepare: Remind yourself of the A-B-C approach and that this can help you tackle the small talk situation.

First, what will be your Aim for this situation? It could be to refuse to even engage in small talk and instead only offer profound or challenging observations as part of establishing your Charisma Effect. But small talk is also part of the oil that keeps human interchange moving smoothly; people with a strong Charisma Effect know how to turn these often irritating situations to their advantage.

A positive Aim might be to:

> Find something really interesting about each person I talk to, no matter how much or how little they say.

This is based on the idea that, for people to find you interesting, they must first experience you as being interested.

A secondary Aim might be to:

Waste no time thinking about myself and instead practise methods of remembering names.

Aim ⟶ Obstacles ⟶ Solutions

What could get in the way of achieving your Aim and how could you plan to overcome it? For example, if you feel you never know what to say, you could prepare a list of topics in advance.

Select: To Be yourself in these small talk situations, you may decide the main behaviour to concentrate on is fluency (see Chapter 2). In this case make sure you have prepared some topics that are non-controversial that you can readily talk about, such as books, climate, family, food being served, movies, new gadgets, pets and so on.

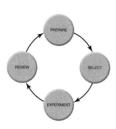

Experiment: You will probably find yourself so busy with finding each person interesting and practising remembering their name that you don't even need your supply of topics to keep things moving. You certainly won't have time to worry about how you look, whether you sound intelligent, talk too much or what to do with your hands.

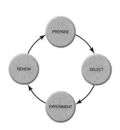

Review: How did it go? Did you manage to find something interesting about each person or were you often distracted or diverted with other people's small talk? How many names can you remember now? Did your name remembering method work well? Which of your prepared topics came up in the conversation or did you manage to mention?

Creating chemistry

Chemistry is the trickiest part of developing your Charisma Effect. Unlike Aim or Be yourself, you cannot 'do' chemistry: it is not a straightforward

chemistry is the trickiest part of developing your Charisma Effect

behaviour you can adopt. Instead, you need to invest in creating the two-way process of building a relationship with your audience.

Now that you have a fuller understanding of what creates Chemistry, there are some practical actions you can take when using the A-B-C approach in any particular situation.

During your interactions with people, try recalling the three core elements (A-I-R): Attention, Interdependence and Rapport. Use them as a mental checklist to assess what is happening *in the moment*, asking:

- 'Am I giving full Attention – what might be stopping me doing that?'
- 'Am I encouraging Interdependence – is there anything getting in the way?'
- 'Am I promoting Rapport – is it happening and if not why not?'

Simply thinking about the A-I-R elements during interactions with other people sharpens your awareness of what is happening. With increased awareness comes a better understanding of ways to positively affect the relationship dynamic.

Once you can comfortably and regularly recall the basic A-I-R elements during actual encounters, the next step is to focus more intensely on one of the three. Which of the three you choose may come down to a combination of intuition, observation of what is happening and feedback. It's a matter of judgement for what seems most needed at that moment.

Since each of these three elements consists of various practical actions you can take, your next choice is selecting an action to experiment with at that moment. For example, if you decide to focus on Interdependence (see Chapter 11), you might select the accept and build approach to experiment with for a while.

Wrap up

If you have read this far, you now have access to the essential tools for transforming your Charisma Effect. In physical fitness training, you can seldom make a huge change in just a few visits to the gym. Instead, it usually works best by taking many small steps that eventually amount to a significant change. Much the same applies to developing your impact with other people. Small steps are usually best.

The Charisma Effect is not a cookbook of best practice so much as a system for continuous personal growth. You will develop your impact by learning and experimenting as you go.

We live in an era that is perhaps most distinctive for its relentlessly accelerating pace of change. We are all part of that experience and if we are not individually to be left behind we must expect to keep changing too.

You already possess a natural ability to deliver some kind of Charisma Effect; it just may not yet be at the level you want. So start experimenting with some of the ideas outlined in this book. Some will work and perhaps surprise you with how effective they are. Others may seem difficult, such as seeking feedback from colleagues, but ultimately all of them can be useful in the right circumstances.

Your Charisma Effect is not a fixed quantity – it has unlimited potential to grow and develop, depending on your commitment to positive action. Once a

your Charisma Effect is not a fixed quantity

year a renowned golfer visits an old professional friend and, as if he were a beginner, says, 'Teach me to play golf.' Like that champion golfer, people who excel and make a strong and lasting impression are willing to keep looking for new ways to improve their impact still further.

Since there is no one right way to make a stunning personal impact, this gives you plenty of scope to use the A-B-C approach to explore this territory. Gradually you will uncover what works for you and what does not. As with any self-development it requires practice.

Improving your Charisma Effect should be high on your agenda, not for selfish reasons, but because it can help you achieve success in your career or whatever you attempt to do.

Of course, the A-B-C approach is not a magic solution, no panacea. It can steer you towards opportunities for making a stronger impression in an age where communicating well has become an essential skill for virtually everyone. As one person who kindly read an early draft of this book commented, 'I've simply become so much more aware of other people's behaviour and I've started to watch my own more carefully.'

Learning to read the communication radar – that is, the relationship dynamic – can be one of the best investments you will ever make.

Good luck!

'If you think you're too small to have an impact, try going to bed with a mosquito in the room.'

Anita Roddick, founder of The Body Shop

At the Charisma Effect website you will find all the additional resources you need, including:

- further reading
- information about workshops
- an ongoing discussion forum for sharing your experiences, asking questions and obtaining helpful answers
- numerous links to organizations and related websites
- videos.

Index